Twayne's New Critical
Introductions to Shakespeare

AS YOU LIKE IT

John Powell Ward

TWAYNE PUBLISHERS · NEW YORK
An imprint of Macmillan Publishing Co.

Published in the United States by Twayne Publishers,
imprint of Macmillan Publishing Co.,
866 Third Avenue, New York, NY 10022

Published simultaneously in Great Britain by
Harvester Wheatsheaf
Campus 400, Maylands Avenue, Hemel Hempstead, Herts.

© 1992 by John Powell Ward
Twayne's New Critical Introductions to Shakespeare, no. 15

Library of Congress Cataloging-in-Publication Data

A CIP catalog record is available from the publisher

ISBN 0–8057–8727–5
ISBN 0–8057–8728–3 (pbk.)

Contents

Replacement 12/01 1

Titles in the Series

GENERAL EDITOR: GRAHAM BRADSHAW

Preface

Down in the forest is a woman. A mind watches her; gets fleeting glimpses of her. The way to her is through the forest, the bush. The way to knowledge is through books. But the books don't satisfy. A lord of Navarre takes a vow to study, and to avoid woman while doing so. He fails, and comes to see that only through woman does he know anything, because only through woman is he wholly orientated to the other, to not-himself. It is the only way the man has. To know is to desire. He must enter into knowledge through the woman, through the brambles and thickets of her bush, her body.

In another place a young man betrays his best friend and his own lady-love, by wooing the best friend's mistress. Foolishly he thought he could conceal this; yet in the forest, which conceals all, he learns that his servant is the woman who despite all had gone on loving him, and that his best friend instantly forgives him.

In another place two lovers, banned from loving by their duke father, flee to the forest. This forest is clear in its detail, and love is celebrated by the brilliant colours on the lovers' clothes and the forest-woman's adornments. But this clarity is not seen by the lovers, nor by another man there, spellbound and turned into an ass; nor by the fairy queen who is spellbound too and falls in love with this ass, loving foolishness through her own. The poet alone imagines it all, giving this dream's airy nothing a local habitation and a name.

In another place a woman herself flees to the forest. She is dressed as a man, and cannot be found by her lover or her father. Only the poet can enter her, enter through her bush to the forest in which she hides but also grows. She can grow; she is not their dream; she is the dream, only, of the poet who enters her and so makes her; finds knowledge in the trees that make the forest, that make the feminine. The poet alone makes that knowledge. The trees themselves tell us this.

In another place, to win a lady 'richly left' a man must choose the honest lead of the rude mechanicals. But she has gone, to her Belmont with its grassy moonlit banks, and when he rejoins her there he doesn't recognise the lawyer who had saved his friend in the city court. He deserves her but doesn't know her. He doesn't know how to go through the woods and the night into her, into her place.

In another place, quite other, a man is tormented by his own ambition, to a point where he learns only from wholly cruel women, or evil ones, shades, equivocators. He cannot go through the wood to the women, they aren't there to find for they disperse before him; their words only break out into clear meaning when the wood itself begins to move. The rooted trees begin to move; reality itself, the feminine mother-reality shifts, it lies like truth and won't stay still.

Thomas Lodge's *Rosalynde. Euphues Golden Legacie*, adapted for the stage by William Shakespeare, was probably first performed in London in 1599. Its somewhat non-committal new title, 'As You Like It', has furrowed foreheads from time to time. Yet since it has become one of the most popular plays ever written, by Shakespeare or anyone else, it could be that the author simply meant what he said by the title, and got it right first time. It is certainly agreed to be a charming if somewhat elusive and tenuous play. Its characters seem, for the most part, happy, yet banished to the forest they live in, and we recall that in *Ulysses* James Joyce named banishment as Shakespeare's lifelong and pervasive obsession. The banishing forces – the

court of Duke Frederick – are distant, but they do hover, if
only in our minds. The play was for a long time not popular. It
was not printed and seldom acted; as far as we know never after
1603 for about 140 years. Conceivably Shakespeare wrote this
talkative play with the new Globe conditions – extended plat-
form for speaking out – very much in mind and it misfired.
In that light it is noteworthy that critics such as Rowse and
Kermode hardly discuss it even when on topic – yet they don't
fault it. It is as though it eludes consciousness, or commands
respect distantly. Yet its popularity remains, on the page and in
performance. Since its author was evidently a man of theatre,
one wonders why so inactive a theme appealed, despite that the
new Globe Theatre was a place of declamation.

Since many contemporary critics won't hear a work praised
or faulted even in the passing *esprit* of a moment, I might
as well say what I think at once. It is a play of the most
extraordinarily elusive subtlety, one of the most meltingly so
ever written; it was intended to delight and it succeeds; it
does, also, contain a greyer, saddening dimension. Attempts to
install this greyer dimension as the reader's chief impression
usually fail, for they would need to convince not only that the
play is sad, which is partly true, but that it is charmless, which
it is manifestly not, at least in the eyes of those who have
reported back on it for centuries. The play has political dimen-
sions, especially in sexual politics, but to make such readings
dominate would itself be a political choice. To emphasise that
dimension – truistically always possible with any phenomenon
whatever – would be to say that it fails (also possible, of
course) to make at least one of its major points: namely, that
life, thank God, is not all politics. One can of course say that
Shakespeare's escapism in avoiding the political is itself political. True, but truistic again. On the other hand, traditional or
conservative emphases on the play's 'intention' (another
critical crux now) seem as equally unpromising. Authorial
intention may lie in making money or having fun, rather
than 'intending' this or that by the text before writing it.
As You Like It is in its own way highly rational, but it is
doubtful if any intention was ever explicit or planned (it
seldom is, for the poet is a blind seer, not a seeing seer);
rather, I would guess, he sensed what he was producing as he

went along, and that he would meet Sidney's (1927) criterion of consciousness-through-delight best by leaving his thoughts and images as tentative in the play as they still were when he came to shape them. For such reasons I prefer Eliade's (1989) phrase 'circulation of sacred energy' (p. 110) to Greenblatt's (1988) echo 'circulation of social energy', very interesting and informative as Greenblatt undeniably is on the social background of this and comparable contemporary plays.

Any black-and-white decision about the play's date – in effect somewhere from 1593 to 1599 – therefore seems less and less appropriate as one approaches the play. The play simply belongs with the period of 'mature comedy' in Shakespeare's early middle age after which he descended – psychologically speaking – into some bewilderment and blackness. Of course a 1593 result would be a surprise, because the play is very sophisticated. But it is not a straight choice of dates. The play could have been sketched or drafted early and written fully later. Rowse (1976) believes Shakespeare wrote the play early for private performance; Dover Wilson (1926) thought, from textual evidence, that the 1599 version was a reworking of an older play. But more interesting is the question of what happened in the 1590s generally. Whether *As You Like It* was effectively written early but not performed until 1599 or so, or whether only a short version was seen by Shakespeare's friends in 1593, then to be expanded when the fuller flowering of mature comedy came at the turn of the century, may not matter. But a possible growth after the sonnets and alongside the history cycle – if that is what happened – may be just worth suggesting as a start.

Lodge's *Rosalynde* must have been always at Shakespeare's elbow, for *As You Like It* is a single-source play. Characters named 'Rosaline' appear in both *Love's Labour's Lost* and *Romeo and Juliet*; possibly the name was on the writer's mind. Equally, Lodge's book was first published in 1590 and then 1592, quite recent if *As You Like It* was written in 1593. But *Rosalynde* was then reprinted in 1596 and 1598. Shakespeare's main changes from Lodge can be listed in summary form. He added Jaques and Touchstone; made the Rosalind–Orlando love more dominant over that of Oliver–Celia and Silvius–Phebe than Lodge did for his corresponding pairs; took out much of Lodge's action including two whole battles; and greatly varied the modes of writing. For, despite his many poems and lucid prose, Lodge's work is largely monotone. This development may have taken years.

In 1593 Shakespeare probably, though not certainly, had written at least a fair number of his sonnets: in Sonnet 86 the Rival Poet, often identified as Marlowe, disappears into the past, and Marlowe was indeed killed in a brawl that year. The whole tenor of the sonnets – almost regardless of what view you take of Shakespeare's sexuality – is of what happens when a young man feels considerable attachment, fatherliness, even necessary subservience, to another young man, the latter acknowledged as being physically attractive. Shakespeare expresses his 'love' of his young man frequently and strongly; his need for his attention, his dejection when his own mistress is apparently disloyal to himself by herself going to that young man. Elizabethan interest in the similarity between the sexes was strong. Meanwhile Christopher Marlowe was writing *Hero and Leander*, a poem with strong bisexual connotations. Shakespeare probably saw the poem long before its later publication. Then comes Marlowe's death, and we recall the three references to Marlowe in *As You Like It* itself (at III, iii, 11–12, III, v, 81–2 and IV, i, 95–101). All three, in context, carry a black shadow of death over them. Meanwhile again, Lodge has dedicated *Rosalynde* to the older Chamberlain, lover of Emilia Lanier, Rowse's choice for Shakespeare's Dark Lady.

It is just possible that all of this, and his dejection at what the sonnets tell, had led Shakespeare at least to rough out a sunny, wistful, 'escapist' and amusing yet somehow also dark and psychologically penetrating play set in a deliberately past setting, his own home of Arden or near, with, however, some melancholic forces pervading its background. This would be the motivation if the play was started early, some time around 1593 or 1594. As Touchstone says (III, iii, 26–7), to find beauty and honesty together is 'to have honey a sauce to sugar', and it is certainly noteworthy how Shakespeare's 'sugred sonnets' as Francis Meres called them, seem of the same grain as *As You Like It*: even-paced; without event or narrative; on love; on time; and foregrounding their language throughout. Shakespeare considered four couples; he looked at the ways pair-bonding can work out. The fancy of Rosalind aping a man in order to teach Orlando to woo was perhaps a fictionalized way of investigating wooing itself; of how he, Shakespeare, had gone wrong with Emilia Lanier, if she it was. Was Shakespeare at last coming out of that trauma? Or had he, anyway, simply found another gratifying lady friend, of however brief duration, and was in some seventh heaven himself? Perhaps evidence may still emerge. Of course, it is surmise. The quotation from Marlowe's poem in *As You Like It* (III, v, 82) is the only direct allusion to a contemporary's work in all of Shakespeare. This would be understandable if Marlowe had just died; less so if it were six years later, but of course Shakespeare didn't quickly forget Marlowe.

However, later events could suggest a different story, further strands adding to what became the play's remarkably easy enlightenment and lightweight maturation. Seymour-Smith (1963) held that all but a dozen of the sonnets were written by 1599, but (for stylistic reasons) as late as possible before that date. In 1594 the Lord Chamberlain's Company was founded with Shakespeare as official playwright. This doubtless brought a new lease of life, a sense of significance and importance for Shakespeare, not to mention the beginnings of more money. Also in 1594, at most a year or two later, appeared the brilliant forest-play *A Midsummer Night's Dream* – brilliant, but surely earlier than *As You Like It* in its lack of a controlling woman figure comparable to the Rosalind figure. And *A Midsummer Night's Dream* may itself have been performed at the wedding of the mother of the Earl of Southampton, himself for many the 'Young Man' of the sonnet sequence. Only in 1596 comes *The Merchant of Venice* with its lead woman growing a little larger, a little more dominant.

In 1595 appeared *Richard II* with its attendant political difficulties of performance. Equally there followed two years later those strongly 'English' performances, the two *Henry IV* plays, with perhaps early thoughts on *Henry V*. The need for tact, to say the least, in political writing, and possibly an inner pressure to stay off it, may have renewed itself. And an alternative emotional direction, as it happens, appeared. In 1596 Shakespeare's son Hamnet died, aged only eleven. The loss of the boy undoubtedly occasioned real grief (cf. *King John*), and the absence of issue from many plays after the historical cycle until the last plays, may be significant. Rosalind's berating of Silvius for wanting to populate the world with 'ill-favour'd children' just could have been a subliminal sad residue, envy at the blessings of others. The play scarcely mentions children elsewhere – nor, admittedly, do the other mature comedies. Yet at once Shakespeare took out a coat-of-arms, and the two things together point to a different emphasis, an urgency to gentleman's status with a continuing line.

When *Henry IV 1* and *2* follow in 1597 they include, along with the significance of Falstaff, a certain creeping back, somewhat, of Warwickshire, and one remembers that in that same year of 1597 Shakespeare bought a grander property in Stratford, New Place, than he had owned hitherto. As early as 1597 too another 'forest' play was probably written, *The Merry Wives of Windsor*, although it was a brief royal-command exercise. Since *Hero and Leander* of Marlowe was published in 1598 the evidence begins to gather, after all, for the later dating of *As You Like It*: 1598 writing, 1599 performance. And, as said before, Lodge's *Rosalynde* was itself reprinted in 1596 and 1598. The buying of New Place may have taken Shakespeare back imaginatively to his home county. Not only was the forest named Arden but Shakespeare's mother too.

Shakespeare needed, perhaps, a non-committal respite from history, politics and socially risky complication. The Earl of Essex went to Ireland early in 1599 to quell the rising there. In January 1599 he had danced with the Queen at a ball. According to Paul Johnson (1974, p. 392), Elizabeth didn't want Essex to lead the Irish campaign, nor did he himself want it. But then he gave the Earl of Southampton – Shakespeare's patron, and almost certainly homosexual, which Elizabeth didn't like – considerably increased power in the invading army. It was only in the summer of 1599 that Essex's record of disobedience to his monarch in Ireland began to come clear. At his return at the end of 1599 Elizabeth was most displeased, even suspecting deliberate rebellion on Essex's part; this of course led to his execution. All this time *As You Like It* had been, presumably, conceived and written; it was then certainly performed. The general unease the playwrights must have been feeling, back indeed to the time of the mysterious death of Marlowe, surely affected Shakespeare; and, while I don't go along with a solely 'escapist' view of the play, it may have seemed a good time to bring to fruition what had long been incubating. It is conceivable that the decision was then taken not simply to write it but to bring it into daylight, to take an easement for himself by attending to a complexity of feelings that had been in him for years regarding women: their place, their nature, their mysterious distance from men, their insepar- able nearness to men, their understanding of men.

It is impossible to say finally. Ruth Nevo's eloquent account (1980) suggests that inventing and defeating the male figure of Falstaff was what gave Shakespeare clear creative space in which to elaborate his major comic heroines, soon to follow. What is certain is that the quotation 'All the world's a stage', or *totus mundus agit histrionem*, became the new Globe Theatre's motto, and that said theatre opened in the year of 1599. Arguably the last of the history cycle, *Henry V*, has a stronger punch with which to open the Globe, and is more explicit about it, but that does not prevent *As You Like It* appearing just before. Further theatrical evidence bears out the general picture. The actor Will Kempe apparently left the Company *early* in 1599 (and he had played Dogberry in *Much Ado About Nothing*, making that play slightly earlier still), and this suggests that Robert Armin, the more melancholy actor, may have played Jaques. There is also the apparent availability of capable boy actors at this time, again suggesting, or at least allowing for, an early draft of the play but a later proper writing. These two things seem to parallel the two chief com- ponents of *As You Like It* – the two fool-intellectuals, and the intersexual cross-dressing and its implications. It points, really, to 1599 – a period of, as it is called, 'mature comedy'. The Arden editor of *Much Ado About Nothing*, along with most others, fairly convincingly sites that play in later 1598, thus leaving space for *As You Like It* early in 1599. In short, these suddenly very happy, woman-centred, lovely, enlarging plays make their appearance between the history cycle and the bitter period of the early seventeenth century.

Even so, what deeply *mattered* to Shakespeare in the play? What is *As You Like It* about? Is it too glib to call it 'happy', 'delightful', etc.? Or could it not be that since nothing human bar instant moments can ever be wholly happy, then the melancholic dimension must pervade too, as Keats thought, to authenticate that very happiness? Or, looking at it differently, is the play perhaps of no intention at all, rather simply grow-ing, as Shakespeare toyed with it here, got brief inspiration there, a bit of dialogue, a song, kept in a drawer perhaps for years against the day of fruition? What day-dreaming was going on, in Shakespeare's mind, to which Lodge's story so exactly appealed? Perhaps we must be content with a pair of possibilities. The characters in the play inhabit, in a sense, Eden. They are banished not from it but to it. Call this escapist perhaps, from the political scene involving Essex and dead Marlowe and Southampton; or call it enlightened, at last an approach to Eve herself and what she silently bore, until the break for sexual freedom became possible. The play's title allows both, and much more besides.

The title – this engagingly pre-empted title – is the other intriguing matter. Much has been said about this title. It may mean 'have it your own way' *or* 'this play is as you have shown you like them' *or* 'I don't give a damn' (Shaw's view) *or* 'this is one for the women' – as *you* but not *you* like it – *or* 'this is one for the judicious among you'. This last would support the view of Salingar (1989) that the late sixteenth-century audience was becoming more and more a critical–professional one, with increasing proportions of, for example, Inns of Court lawyers. For them, Touchstone's 'let the forest judge' would have had a nice ambivalence. Intriguingly, our understanding of the title thereby becomes one of the things to which that same title may be applied.

The common, if commonly unspoken, view is that *As You Like It* should be thought of with the play's epilogue in mind: 'I charge you, O women, for the love you bear to men, to like as much of this play as please you'. Yet if we count the later tragic closures as also putative epilogues to the audiences ('We that are young/Shall never see so much, nor live so long'), we shall surely feel it as likely that the epilogue came out of the title, rather than the reverse.

It is even possible – this is quite serious – that a Globe manager-actor sent a note over to Will at Blackfriars asking for a name for the latest folio the bard had sent in. Will was busy that week, what with the Globe itself about to open and Will Kempe just leaving and being replaced, and the whole new part of Touchstone superimposed on Lodge just for this one man! So he just scrawled, in effect, 'no preference' across it and sent the tricksy slave back. It may even have become a Company joke, as the subtitle of his next comedy, *Twelfth Night*, might suggest.

And, with such a title, such an inactive play and such an elusive history, criticism is left with a receding target. On paper, few parts of the story are necessary to other parts. The banishments are not necessary to the wooing, or wrestling to songs, or even a forest to a Jaques-figure. There is no historical narrative or tragic curve. This makes any character-criticism tenuous, for (even suspending current critical suspicion of Bradleism anyway) we can't go all the way into 'characters' who do nothing. Character and personality are formed out of action, occupation, family and community as much as by what is innate. But little or none of these things is present in the Forest of Arden. Attempts have been made by some to elaborate court–country distinctions, but this can bear only so much weight. Even more desperately, we are told that the 'social class' of Rosalind and Corin differs and that such is essential to a reading of the play. Such critics are clearly not Marxists, for Marx believed that all activity could be traced to the basic struggle for ownership of the means of material production. There is no such struggle in Arden, for all are provided for, and no one has any subsistence or shelter problem whatever.

We are not offered characters, but aspects of character. We can't ignore, or indeed refuse to enquire about, the prototype in each case and their local realisation here: the restless, pained melancholic, the terse back-seat girl companion, the unenquiring handsome young man, the neurotic usurper. But equally we cannot round them up into full people with histories, networks of unmentioned motives or the inward soliloquies which Lodge included and Shakespeare omitted. The question 'was Rosalind a virgin?' (and I do ask it; see below) may be interesting to the prurient and, certainly, throws different lights over events according to how we make answer. But it still can't be settled on either way without desensitising the play's imaginative subtlety alarmingly. It lingers in the mind longer than the question of how many children Lady Macbeth had, but can still only be postulated, as a notion, a whimsy or a serious moral inference.

We can only say what we see. I myself see a sudden arena of peace. Politics and acrimony have themselves been banished in Act I; in Act II a harmless moaner has his interesting say and falls silent, and after that we are left in a glade from which the undergrowth has been cleared, with two people talking about love. Of course, a marshmallow reading will simply dehydrate the play, but equally attempts to see it as 'really' a nasty and threatening stew of bourgeois hang-ups simply won't survive; the material just isn't there, a fact one discovers by looking for it, title or no title. Rather, the presence of what is able to be spoilt, what risks we would take by assuming the play's real happiness could last for ever, beyond the play's end – that, surely, is what the loud melancholy of Jaques and wistful melancholy of Rosalind get across.

How it all amounts to an aesthetic unity describable in prose summary I haven't, after many months thinking about it, been able to fathom; but this power both to elude and satisfy at once is the play's unique quality. There is nothing one would want cut or rearranged. The critical question – I still hanker after saying 'mystery' – is how a play drawn from a single source could then embody something so delicate and tenuous, while still so totally absorbing one's attention. Of course it is something to do with Sir Philip Sidney and art lying (pun) in concealing art, but analysis of that is not an option because analysis of it would kill it in the act of exposure. It is also – and the title includes this suggestion – an invitation to make our own play from its parts. I say 'make' rather than the fashionable word 'construct' because the engineering industry would be out of place in the forest, and our dreamy shapings really arise from where our own half-remembered pasts link to the half-suggested characters and leafy corners in the play itself. Neither has boundaries, so they merge easily but remain shadowy, floating, imprecise.

For like reasons, after a long preamble about the play's reception over four hundred years (I apologise, but it is fascinating and critically informative), I have tried to follow the play's spirit by writing not with six or seven heavyweight chapter-headings, but twenty-five or so short sections. If the result hangs together like a vulnerable molecular chain (or the one round Orlando's neck) that will be at least something. My preamble is rather longer than usual for such studies, but the way attention to Jaques and Rosalind has relentlessly grown through different eras seems to me most instructive as to how we see the play now and might see it anew.

It remains only to express gratitude to those numerous family members, friends, colleagues, publishers and others who have helped in the writing of this book, and to express regret both that it is impossible to name them all and that their various good influences will have long since so dispersed themselves through what follows that it would be equally impossible to trace them all. I must, however, mention one person, this book's dedicatee, my former tutor who taught me about Shakespearian comedy thirty years ago and whose ideas and insights I have found myself remembering as though it were yesterday. However, any distortions of these memories and indeed all these influences are, needless to say, my own responsibility. Thanks to him also for, in effect, a seminar–lunch a few months ago when I was half-way through drafting this book. It was of the greatest value.

Finally, there is as always the opposition. The Protestant anti-theatre diatribe *Th' Overthrow of Stage-Playes* appeared in 1599, probable year of this play's writing and first production. It was written by Dr John Rainolds, Master of Corpus Christi College, Oxford. Did the learned doctor notice that his last name anagrams 'Rosalind'? It seems somehow to compromise his position, not that Shakespeare knew it. But of that make What You Will.

John Powell Ward

The stage history and
the critical reception

'Is poetry a true thing?' asked Audrey, a little suspicious. 'Is *criticism* a true thing?' wrote Keats (his emphasis), on his copy of Dr Johnson's note on *As You Like It*. True or not, criticism of this play was a long time coming. There was little sustained response before the nineteenth century, and what occurs then has a wonderful extravagance of its own. Only in our own post-war period has professional attention to the comedies really started.

Yet fascinating bits-and-pieces have gathered; there are early puzzlements and passing remarks, actresses' reminiscences, notable performances, intrigued theatregoers' responses, scholarly minutiae, and stagings in unlikely places. Who or what Rosalind really is, whether the play is best performed outdoors, and what to make of the enigmatic Jaques, come to the surface here and there. And *As You Like It* has a remarkable performance record. It is one of the top two or three for performance-frequency at Stratford, and probably most other places, out of all the Shakespeare plays (Reynolds, 1988, p. 61; Lathem, 1975, pp. lxxvi–xci).

It started auspiciously, being written perhaps for the opening of the Globe Theatre itself. Yet we then have no real record of

any performance for the next 140 years. That is unlikely to re-
flect reality, but certainly the play seems not to have come back
into favour when the theatres reopened after the Restoration.
So the first detailed description we have is of Charles Johnson's
bastardised rewriting 'Love in a Forest' in 1723, which omitted
Touchstone and others, but incorporated voluminous material
from other plays and, notably, married off Jaques to Celia.
(George Sand did the same a hundred years later.) Only
fourteen years before Johnson, Nicholas Rowe had seemed
impressed but puzzled: 'The Conversation of . . . Rosalind in
As You Like It has much Wit and Sprightliness all along . . . the
melancholy of Jaques is as singular as it is diverting' (Vickers,
1974–81, vol. II, pp. 195–6). Charles Gildon, a year after Rowe,
is equally intrigued at this unlikely piece of theatre: 'This story
has nothing Dramatic in it, yet *Shakespeare* has made as good
use of it as possible'. The sermons-in-stones speech is 'full
of moral reflections', Orlando and Adam are touching, and
'*Rosalind's* Character of a Man in Love is very pretty' (Vickers,
1974–81, vol. II, pp. 243–4). So the depressive–intellectual
theme, the talk theme, the transsexual theme and the lack-of-
action theme get noted early, as the things to be expanded on in
later criticism.

Whether the first poets made much of it is impossible to say.
Milton's snake slinking into the undergrowth (*Paradise Lost*
IX, 784) seems cognate with *AYLI* IV, iii, 110–13, and a play
with an old Adam in a place named almost wilfully to echo
'Garden of Eden' just may have struck him. The Earl of
Rochester's couplet on Charles II ('He never said a foolish
thing/Nor ever did a wise one') does feel enriched by Touchstone's sardonic observation about action and speech near the
play's start: 'The more pity that fools may not speak wisely what
wisemen do foolishly'. More clearly derivative might be Brisk
in William Congreve's *The Double-Dealer* – 'Paints d'ye say?
– why she lays it on with a trowel' (III, x, 96–7) – which echoes
exactly if more cosmetically Celia's praise of her fool's sly
euphuism at *AYLI* I, ii, 98. Such stray shots could mean the
play was alive in the study if not on stage: but this is surmise.

Early in the eighteenth century production of Shakespeare
rose markedly, reaching 40 per cent of all performances in
London in 1740–1. These included a highly successful *As You*

Like It that winter, very probably for the first time since the Restoration (Vickers, 1974–81, vol. III, p. 13). Jaques was played by James Quin. Elizabeth Montague wrote of him that she 'never heard anything spoke with such command of voice and action as the seven stages [*sic*] of man . . . he spoke the slipper'd pantaloon just like my uncle Clark' (Climenson, pp. 47–8). Quin played Jaques in Dublin again the next year. The ages/stages modification looks forward to Wordsworth's Immortality Ode and to the twentieth century's absorption with the play's emphasis on time.

In May 1757 Peg Woffington, long a rival Rosalind to that of Mrs Pritchard, made her last appearance. In the Epilogue, at 'as had beards that pleased me', she apparently screamed 'O God! O God!', rushed off stage and collapsed, the audience applauding the whole way out. Only 44, she lived a mere skeleton for just two more years. The highly successful Mrs Siddons twice tried Rosalind in the mid-1780s, but this queen of tragedy couldn't make the transition. Anne Seward wrote: 'The playful scintillations of colloquial wit, which most strongly mark that character, suit not the dignity of the Siddonian form and countenance. Then her dress was injudicious. The scrupulous prudery of decency, produced an ambiguous vestment, that seemed neither male nor female' – an outcome our own era would approve. Siddons's better success as Rosalind herself (i.e. not Ganymede) is instructive. One of those 'rays of exquisite and original discrimination, which her genius so perpetually elicits, shone out on her first rushing upon the stage in her own resumed person and dress'. She 'bent the knee' to her father, 'fell into the arms' of Orlando and gave the 'I am yours' (V, iv, 115–16) to the Duke with 'the tender joy of filial love' and to lover-boy himself with 'the whole soul of enamoured transport' (all quoted from Salgado, 1975, pp. 161–8). The doubleness of the comic character (a repeated twentieth-century critical theme) frustrated Siddons perhaps, but we also see here the beginnings of Rosalind the Heavenly, who recurs throughout nineteenth-century responses altogether. However, there were many successful Rosalinds at this time, as Agnes Lathem (1975) has reported, and this play was performed at Drury Lane in the years 1775 to 1815 more than any other by Shakespeare.

The scholars still weren't saying much. They respected the play, it would seem, but their references tended to be brief and textual, as though the play raised risky implications, or else its literary authenticity could by now be taken for granted. In 1747 the eminent editor William Warburton traced Touchstone's 'seventh cause' speech back to the 'very ridiculous' treatise of Vicentio Saviolo of 1594 – incidentally dating our play after that date, unless that material were later written in. In 1748 John Upton, Prebendary of Rochester Cathedral, attending to puns, noted the goat tie-up with 'capricious' at III, iii, 6, and Jaques's comment about 'Jove in a thatched house'. Concluding they are 'lascivious' he added only that 'to explain puns is almost as unpardonable as to make them' (Vickers, 1974–81, vol. III, pp. 234, 304). In 1754 Zachary Grey opted simply to summarise the *Tale of Gamelyn* as a source for *As You Like It* and in 1767 Richard Farmer ridiculed Grey's suggestion. As late as 1795 in the *Critical Review* William Guthrie confined himself to explaining the meaning of 'quintain'. In 1770 Paul Hiffernan had proposed a temple to Shakespeare containing about fifteen scenes, including Touchstone and Rosalind 'berhiming' her name.

The few comments of a more human weighting are still usually cursory. In 1748 Peter Whelby, a Fellow of St John's, Cambridge, compared the 'sequester'd stag' scene (*AYLI* II, i, 25–66) to its source in Virgil's *Aeneid* (VII, 500ff.) to Shakespeare's advantage. 'What an exquisite Image this of dumb Distress' (Vickers, 1974–81, vol. III, p. 284) – but there is no wider comment, or sense of the Lord's feeling of the scene's comedy. In 1759 Thomas Wilkes, like Rowe fifty years before, again records briefly – and sincerely enough – Orlando's touching care for Adam. The late eighteenth century's increased concern with the 'deserving poor', articulated in such as Gray and Crabbe, may have found a chord in these scenes.

Samuel Johnson himself, giving barely ten lines to the play, confides rather differently: 'I know not how the ladies will approve the facility with which both *Rosalind* and *Celia* give away their hearts. To *Celia* much may be forgiven for the heroism of her friendship' (Johnson, 1908, p. 86). This, with Johnson's regret that we were not given the full discussion between Jaques and the newly converted Duke Frederick at the end, gives an eighteenth-century overcast to the whole approach, captured perhaps in Steevens's contemporary view on why men dominate in Shakespeare: '[it is] by that natural pre-eminence which they possess in the unavoidable course of things' (Vickers, 1974–81, vol. v, p. 499). There had been some unease about Jaques, for others too felt that he and Adam were not sufficiently involved in the final catastrophe: only Johnson would have altered the play's course the other way.

Valuable and rare attention was given to Jaques at about this time, in a detailed analysis from William Richardson in 1774. It focuses economically on what makes readers take sides on the subject:

> Jaques, avoiding society, and burying himself in the lonely forest, seems to act inconsistently with his constitution. He possesses sensibility; sensibility begets affection; and affection begets the love of society. But Jaques is unsocial. Can these inconsistent qualities be reconciled? or has Shakespeare exhibited a character of which the parts are incongruous and discordant?

On the contrary, argues Richardson, Shakespeare has made a complex character by balancing in it the qualities of melancholy and misanthropy. Melancholy comes from 'the sorrow excited by repulsed and languishing affection', misanthropy from 'the disappointment of selfish appetites . . . melancholy is amiable and benevolent, and wishes mankind would reform: misanthropy is malignant, and breathes revenge'. As a result it can be said:

> this mixture of melancholy and misanthropy in the character is more agreeable to human nature than the representation of either of the extremes. . . . As benevolence and sensibility are manifest in the temper of Jaques, we are not offended with his severity. . . . His sadness, of a mild and gentle nature, recommends him to our regards; his humour amuses. (in J.R. Brown, 1979, pp. 29–30)

And yet, in the very years when Johnson wrote, the mature comedies were beginning quietly to remain in the theatregoers' consciousnesses. This, no doubt, led to the forty-year popularity of *As You Like It* at Drury Lane mentioned earlier. In 1761 George Coleman had recorded that 'within all our memories they [four comedies including *As You Like It*] have been ranked among the most popular Entertainments of the Stage'. Five years later Bishop Richard Hurd states that 'Shakespeare had, indeed, set the example of something like pastoral drama in our language; and in his Winter's Tale, As Ye [*sic*] Like It, and some other of his pieces has enchanted every body with his natural sylvan manners, and sylvan scenes' (Vickers, 1974–81, vol. IV, p. 443; vol. V, p. 257). The forest looms, yet Shakespeare's 'good sense' constrains his use of pastoral to the enrichment only of the comedy itself. A comment by David Erskine Baker (1764) gives unreserved praise: 'It is, perhaps, the truest pastoral drama that ever was written; nor it is ever seen without pleasure to all present. In the closet it gives equal delight, from the beauty and simplicity of the poetry' (in J.R. Brown, 1979, p. 25). Baker singles out Jaques's seven ages speech for special commendation. The tendency to praise this play without really knowing why pervades the tradition, with notable exceptions, until the middle of our own century.

The eighteenth century ends, certainly, with a much fuller treatment of the play, for almost the first time – hardly promising, though one can scarcely refrain from citing it. Walter Whiter's *A Specimen of a Commentary on Shakespeare* (1794) is in two parts: I Notes on *As You Like It*; II 'An Attempt To Explain and Illustrate various Passages, on a New Principle of Criticism, derived from Mr Locke's Doctrine of the Association of Ideas' (Vickers, 1974–81, vol. VI, p. 606). Such points forward to the exciting dangers of interactive-discourse analysis of our own time.

The Romantic period began to see much increased interest in *As You Like It*, as indeed in Shakespeare generally, but from an unexpected source. Late eighteenth-century poets had used it only sporadically. William Blake's *Songs of Innocence and Experience* were matched with passages from the play by the Royal Shakespeare Company for their production programme in 1990 at the Barbican, but no evidence for direct influence was given; however, the first etching in Blake's sequence *The Gates of Paradise* (1793) is called 'I found him under a tree', a direct lift from *AYLI* iii, ii, 230–1. How typical of Blake to be the lonely first in what clearly became an 'under-the-tree' motif in much nineteenth-century writing. Meanwhile the Reverend William Bowles, made famous by Coleridge, used the Arden-forest material in his long poem 'Shakespeare', said by Coleridge to be 'sadly unequal' to Bowles's other work. No, the Shakespeare revival came, via Hazlitt, from the German Romantics, in light of which it is possibly curious that Coleridge, huge Germanist apologist as he was, was more concerned as to how *As You Like It* could have been thought of by a man. Coleridge adds little more than a whimsy about the scene that so fascinated the eighteenth-century critics. 'Think of the scene between [Adam] and Orlando; and think again, that the actor of that part had to carry the author of that play in his arms!' (in Coleridge, 1971, pp. 131, 132; there is an old tradition, not without supporting evidence, that the part of Adam was played by Shakespeare himself, Dowden, 1911, p. 669). Coleridge did, certainly, more than once note the spirit-of-the-whole nature of the play's title, contrasting it with the one-man titles of so many of Shakespeare's plays, and so raising again, by implication, the centrality or otherwise of Rosalind (1960, vol. 1, pp. 52, 206, plus letter citations too numerous to list here). Far more significantly however, the German critic A.W. Schlegel had presented his lectures on drama at the turn of the century and William Hazlitt made excerpts from them the basis of his introduction to his *Characters of Shakespeare's Plays* of 1818.

It is exactly Schlegel's romantic sense that appeals to Hazlitt, in contrast to the propriety and balance of Johnson. Johnson is quoted to equal length but to his disadvantage. 'The shifting shape of fancy, the rainbow hues of things, made no impression on him.' Schlegel by contrast praises Shakespeare for his passion, and furthermore in comedy too, which he (Shakespeare) places 'on an equal elevation [with the tragic], and [which] possesses equal extent and profundity'. What follows could be on *As You Like It* itself. 'He plays with love like a child, and his songs are breathed out like melting sighs' (in Hazlitt, 1818, pp. xiv–xvii).

This ethereally accurate phrasing seems to be behind Hazlitt's own comments on the play itself.

It is the most ideal of any of this author's plays. It is a pastoral drama, in which the interest arises more out of the sentiments and characters than out of the actions or situations. It is not what is done, but what is said, that claims our attention. Nursed in solitude, 'under the shade of melancholy boughs', the imagination grows soft and delicate, and the wit runs riot in idleness, like a spoiled child, that is never sent to school . . . the very air of the place seems to breathe a spirit of philosophical poetry; to stir the thoughts, to touch the heart with pity, as the drowsy forest rustles to the sighing gale. (pp. 305–6)

'Not what is done but what is said . . .'; we go back to Gildon, and forward to Harold Jenkins, via Matthew Arnold (who perhaps disapproved as we shall see), Agnes Mure Mackenzie and others. The under-the-tree theme reappears, and the shifting breeze of Arden forest becomes the play's heart, whence it will vie with Rosalind herself. In 1925, for example, after more fulsome Rosalind praise, E.K. Chambers wrote: 'And yet, splendid as it is, there is an even greater part in *As You Like It*. And that is the part of the Forest of Arden.' The question of which matters most, Rosalind or some atmosphere-in-general, underlies virtually all *As You Like It* criticism. For Hazlitt, Jaques is actionless in consequence. 'Jaques is the only purely contemplative character in Shakespeare. He thinks, and does nothing' (p. 306). Hazlitt didn't then consult his friend Charles Lamb, whose *Tales From Shakespeare* (written with his sister Mary) had been published in 1807, but whose real god was the seventeenth-century writer Richard Burton. The latter's analysis of melancholy, albeit twenty years after, is where we might best look for clues to Jaques. But Hazlitt's interest lies not in melancholy but in love, and that keeps him clear of too total a fragrant-as-a-flower Rosalind: 'her tongue runs the faster to conceal the pressure at her heart. She talks herself out of breath, only to get deeper in love' (p. 307) – see *As You Like It* III, ii, 178–246.

Interestingly, Hazlitt also reports of *As You Like It* that 'hardly any of Shakespeare's plays contain more quoted passages, or that have become proverbial'. If this is true, at a time when Shakespeare generally became more and more popular, it suggests again an embryonic growth in the public consciousness of this play long before the appearance of a fully articulated criticism. The matters that are later debated already intrigue: the lack of action, the role of Rosalind, Jaques, the forest, the sprightly dialogue. And Shakespeare was certainly becoming more popular. As Elizabeth Jenkins (1961) put it, writing of Jane Austen, 'one may judge how well the revivers of Shakespeare had done their work when in 1813 Henry Crawford was to say: "Shakespeare one gets acquainted with without knowing how. He is part of an Englishman's constitution."' (p. 140). On comedy in particular Peter Raby, writing of the actress Harriet Smithson Berlioz (wife of the composer), puts it more guardedly, but excepts *As You Like It* itself: 'The taste for Shakespearian comedy had not yet [in the 1820s] been fully reawakened . . . *As You Like It* was frequently played, but in general Shakespearean comedy was looked on as suitable material for musical elaboration' (Raby, 1982, pp. 36–7) – including, all too frequently, the Cuckoo Song from *Love's Labour's Lost*, tacked on to our play at will since a hundred years before.

This awakening interest took a number of forms. One, simply, was the ripple outwards of productions into the provinces and abroad, although that of course applied to Shakespeare generally. But comedy was a large beneficiary. London theatre companies increasingly performed Shakespeare in Paris in the 1820s. Two somewhat amazing fictions result perhaps from this Paris period. The later, and still better known, is the mid-century attempt by the French woman novelist George Sand to follow Charles Johnson in rewriting the play, marrying Jaques off to Celia at the end. The dissatisfaction with Jaques's structural treatment, mentioned earlier, begins to be pressing, and is perhaps not fully answered until Northrop Frye's theory of comedy in the middle of the twentieth century. Even more intriguing is the first novel by the French writer and artist Théophile Gautier, *Mademoiselle de Maupin* of 1835, written when he was 24. The novel wholly and explicitly centres on *As You Like It*, the play itself being acted out in the grounds of the country house in the novel's later stages. The phenomenon is informative, for Gautier is sexually explicit in ways the British audience was manifestly not ready for: indeed the novel was shocking enough in France. The young poet d'Albert and his mistress Rosette both fall in love with a page-boy, who turns out to be a woman. But earlier, the poet had felt his (her) legs on his as they approached close while riding side-saddle, and the truth is revealed when the 'page', stunned in a riding accident, is found to be a woman by the discovery, under her clothing, of a breast, no less. Rosalind in Shakespeare is given no such appendages.

Yet, despite the explicit sexuality, Gautier speaks of the actual play itself in just the terms we find later in so many nineteenth- and early twentieth-century British responses. A longish excerpt is needed (from Chapter xi) for the effect to be gathered:

> As you read this strange play, you feel yourself transported into another world, of which you still have some vague recollection. You no longer know if you're alive or dead, dreaming or waking; graceful figures smile at you sweetly, and send you a friendly good-morning as they pass; you feel moved and disturbed as you see them, as if, as you turned the corner of the path, you suddenly encountered your ideal, or the forgotten phantom of your first mistress suddenly rose before you. Springs are flowing, humming their stifled lamentations; the wind is stirring before the secular trees in the ancient forest over the head of the old exiled duke, with companionate sighs; and when the melancholy Jaques sends his philosophic complaints down the stream with the willow leaves, it seems to you that you yourself are speaking, and that the most secret, the most obscure corner of your heart is revealed and illuminated. (1981 edition, p. 229)

We begin to wonder whether, including across the Victorian decades ahead, these breezes and airs and fragrances are an extended allegory for the unspeakableness of sex itself, with the forest as genitalia and Rosalind a sprite-Eros within it. Conversely the latter could mean, following Foucault, that sex was being increasingly spoken all the time. It would explain a trend of criticism, on into the mid-1920s, to which we shall come.

Meanwhile, more mundanely, back in Britain *As You Like It* had appeared at the Theatre Royal in Bath, just once, in 1807. In the 1836-7 season the play was Bath's only production, and it appeared there again in 1864 for the tercentenary celebrations. *As You Like It* was produced in Leicester four times from 1850 to 1895. Helena Faucit (Lady Martin) did a triumphant Rosalind in Glasgow, Edinburgh and Dublin on numerous occasions, indeed until her years might have advised against it. In the very first year of the Shakespeare Theatre at Stratford-on-Avon in 1879 a real stag (recently killed but quickly stuffed) was dragged across the stage in a scene done with full ceremony. The tradition continued until 1919, when it ceased only with great protest. Back on stage, the play had reached Melbourne by 1843 (four performances by 1861) and by 1897 the Women's Club at Denver, Colorado – outdoors.

London productions of course continued, and increased too. The poet William Wordsworth probably didn't see one, when his sister Dorothy went to Drury Lane in 1797, because he did not then care for theatre. Indeed he never mentions *As You Like It* explicitly in his work. The more intriguing then that there is a sort of *As You Like It* subtext surfacing here and there in his poetry, and I suggest it shows, again, the deep current running for this elusive and then-questionable play which a thinking and feeling public was coming to terms with. Wordsworth was, of course, writing fifteen years before Hazlitt's breakthrough. In *The Prelude* (1805), x, 70, where Wordsworth recalls the French Revolution massacres, we read suddenly that 'the horse is taught his manage'. As Bate points out (1989, p. 113), it seems an odd phrase until we remember that it is from Orlando's complaint about his brother's treatment of him (*AYLI* i, i, 12). Wordsworth's ensuing lines about the wheel of time, 'year after year, the tide returns again,/day follows day' seem to echo Celia near the start and Touchstone as Jaques reports him in ii, vii, 12ff. It is curiously irrelevant, until we recall Wordsworth's Immortality Ode itself, and its seven (actually four) stages of the child's growth to manhood and 'palsied Age'. Since, earlier in the poem, Wordsworth had with equal abruptness recalled 'But there's a tree, of many,

one,/A single Tree that I have looked upon', another *Prelude*
passage becomes relevant:

> When here and there about the grove of oaks
> Where was my bed, an acorn from the trees
> Fell audibly, and with a startling sound.
>
> (1805, I, 92–4)

This also seems to recall Celia's news about finding Orlando
in the forest – the same phrase used by Blake – 'I found him
under a tree like a dropped acorn'. The fact suddenly swells up
in front of us, that the one single citing of this play in all
Wordsworth's prose is of a single tree too: Oliver's 'Under an
oak, whose boughs were moss'd with age,/And high top bald
with dry antiquity' (*AYLI* IV, iii, 104–5). (It occurs in 'Select
Views': Appendix II to the poet's *A Guide through the District
of the Lakes*.) My hunch, not provable, is that the play lies
behind the poem 'Nutting' and, perhaps, some of Wordsworth's 'Lucys' and 'solitary reapers'.

The under-the-tree theme then recurs repeatedly and phallic-
ally through Thomas Hardy to Robert Frost. I emphasise,
perhaps overemphasise, Wordsworth at this point because of
what is to follow. What happens in the nineteenth century after
Wordsworth, very clearly from the evidence, is two things: a
clear increase in articulated response to *As You Like It* by
women, and a period – that of 'high seriousness' – when it may
have been treated with contrasting suspicion and some dis-
approval. Wordsworth's poetry is the moment for *As You Like
It* when longing for it and guilt at it combine in the turning-
inwardness from Shakespeare's externalised Arden to the
psyche as where nature is both benign and morally severe at
once. Indeed a remark by Oscar Wilde nearly ninety years
later, in 1889, and four years after he had seen an outdoor *As
You Like It* he greatly enjoyed, ties Wordsworth to this play
explicitly. 'Wordsworth went to the lakes, but he was never a
lake poet. He found in stones the sermons he had already
hidden there.' It comes from Wilde's essay 'The Decay of
Lying', and the point is germane to the truth-feigning theme of
the play, a point also made by Francis Bacon not long after its
writing, and to which we shall return. Wilde called Gautier's

novel the 'holy writ of beauty', a phrase he incidentally also used for Pater's *Renaissance*.

Thomas Hardy carries on the under-the-tree theme and the compulsive approach to women, going on from three poems he wrote after seeing a performance of *As You Like It* in the 1860s. This was right in the thick of the askance look toward the play by some, as we shall see. Hardy's biographer Robert Gittings says the poet saw Mrs Scott-Siddons (granddaughter of the tragic actress) play Rosalind at the Haymarket in 1867. But the longer poem 'The Two Rosalinds' refers to 'eighteen sixty-three', and elsewhere Hardy refers to having seen the actress Helena Faucit, an important figure in the play's story as we shall see below. However, according to Gittings, Hardy saw Scott-Siddons on 8 April 1867 in her stage début. He was taken by her 'neat, pretty figure' and the tights in which she slotted it, in 'a part beloved for that reason by all right-thinking Victorian gentlemen' (Gittings, 1978, pp. 144–5). Hardy added the sonnet 'To An Impersonator of Rosalind' two weeks later, and 'To An Actress' the same year. 'The Two Rosalinds' claims, internally, to be 'some forty years' later – quite probably correctly, knowing Hardy – and alludes to a bad performance contrasting the wonderful earlier one, and a 'hag' who claims to have played it – though certainly not the ageing Helena Faucit, who went on playing Rosalind for so long. The later of the 'Rosalind' poems is much the longer, but both refer to, and quote, the play itself. But the repeat of the name, 'Rosalind', in the title is what stays with us.

The date is important, for if 1867 is correct it was only a year before Hardy probably first conceived *Under The Greenwood Tree* (Gittings, 1978, p. 218), a novel whose ancestry is suggested not only by its title. Another Hardy biographer, Michael Millgate, alludes to that novel's 'minimal plot-line' and suggests its unusual beauty derives precisely from its 'lack of story' (Millgate, 1982, p. 136). The novel was completed in 1871. Hardy by then may well have internalised *As You Like It* quite deeply. If he had, then again the play's silent spread is found in the nineteenth-century's response, the sermons in stones now giving way to the solitary's sadness before both nature and inner desire.

But what then did nineteenth-century women begin to say?

A number wrote of the play in the later years of the century, with Mary Cowden Clarke and Mrs Leigh Elliott prominent. Their forerunners had included two formidable women who both wrote in the 1830s. First was Mrs Anna Jameson with her studies of most of Shakespeare's women characters. Mrs Jameson placed Rosalind among the 'characters of intellect' along with Beatrice, Isabella and Portia, in contrast to those of 'passion' who included Juliet, Ophelia, Viola and Miranda. Mrs Jameson is critical enough, seeing Rosalind as 'superior [to Beatrice] as a woman, but as a dramatic character inferior in force'. But the real difficulty lay in identifying Rosalind's actual characteristics. She is 'so exquisitely blended, that on any attempt to analyze them, they seem to escape us'. A common response; but what then do we do? Compare her, of course, to 'the silvery summer-clouds, to a mountain streamlet – to the May-woman, flush with opening flowers and roseate dews' etc., etc., 'fresh as the morning, sweet as the dew-awakened blossoms', and so on and so on (Jameson, 1832, pp. 76–7).

Comments like this then pervade talk of *As You Like It* for over a hundred years. I take them very seriously and will return to them as we gather their blooms. Jameson was no drip; she starts her book with a terse fictional dialogue about the woman's right to be a critic at all. The other woman to write extensively on the play was the actress Helena Faucit (Lady Martin), whose Rosalind was her most successful part in an always outstanding career. Faucit first played Rosalind in 1839 when only 22 herself. She felt she didn't do it full justice, but still wrote to Robert Browning a letter no less than sixty pages long, devoted entirely to going stage-by-stage through the details of this single part in a way fascinating to put beside a comparable recent statement by the actress Juliet Stevenson, the 1986 RSC Rosalind in Adrian Noble's production. Faucit wrote about all her major parts (Browning commonly the recipient) and acted Rosalind frequently for nearly forty years. Faucit must be cited at length. A little before saying (for Rosalind) 'O happiness beyond belief, O rapture irrepressible!' on learning that Arden now contains Orlando, here is her considered survey of the wooing scenes:

Those forest scenes between Orlando and herself are not, as a comedy actress would be apt to make them, merely pleasant fooling. At the core of all that Rosalind says and does, lies a passionate love as pure and all-absorbing as ever swayed a woman's heart. Surely it was the finest and boldest of all devices, one on which only a Shakespeare could have ventured, to put his heroine into such a position that she could, without revealing her own secret, probe the heart of her lover to the very core, and thus assure herself that the love that possessed her being was as completely the master of his. Neither could any but Shakespeare have so carried out this daring design, that the woman thus rarely placed for gratifying the impulses of her own heart, and testing the sincerity of her lover's, should come triumphantly out of the ordeal, charming us during the time of probation, by her wit, her fancy, by her pretty womanly waywardness. . . . Hence it is that Orlando finds the spell which 'heavenly Rosalind' had thrown around him, drawn hourly closer and closer, he knows not how, while at the same time he has himself been winning his way more and more into his mistress's heart. Thus, when at last Rosalind doffs her doublet and hose, and appears arrayed for her bridal, there seems nothing strange or unmeet in this somewhat sudden consummation of what has been in truth a lengthened wooing. The actress will, in my opinion, fail signally in her task, who shall not suggest all this. (Faucit, 1841, pp. 236–7)

Faucit didn't know Lodge, then; and, because it puts us off, it is easy to miss the measured phrasing and judicious care taken over what is said. What Faucit is doing, in reality, is to leave the big question – of Rosalind's relation to Arden – hanging in the air. As with Jameson's version, Rosalind still has no characteristics. Yet her effect is undeniable, so all this about daring and spell-binding and lover's heart and the rest has to go in if what we instinctively explore now – strategy and sex – is to be avoided, as in the Victorian age it had to be. Jameson, with no other option, ties her across to nature; Faucit keeps her human but impossibly idealised. And yet there is no need to be cynical. The play *does* walk an astonishing tightrope of near-ethereal airy balance, by painting a 'forest' it doesn't describe and a love-match through Ganymede's disguise never quite present. Jameson and Faucit at least tried to convey *that*, to say *something*, and we can be grateful for the witness they give us as to what, then, was the limit of articulation.

For – and this is the other main theme here – 'high seriousness' was not far ahead. Charlotte Brontë, perhaps surprisingly, weighs in early. 'The finest passages are always the purest, the bad are invariably revolting; you will never wish to read them over twice. Omit the comedies of Shakespeare and the "Don Juan"' (Houghton, 1957, p. 357). Of course, *As You Like It* is Shakespeare's least bawdy comedy. But its other questionable feature, transvestitism, is also held warily distant, at least before Wilde and Shaw and Swinburne. Again and again an actress or critic will make clear that their Rosalind was pure girl unsullied. But the 1860s are the low period. In 1864, the tercentary year no less, the Bath production already mentioned was a failure, and the 16-year-old Edmund Gosse, in London the same year, heard an evangelical preacher call Shakespeare 'a departed sinner'. An eminent man of letters like John Morley, reviewing Swinburne, wrote that 'No language is too strong to condemn the mixed vileness and childishness of depicting the spurious passion of a putrescent imagination, the unnamed lusts of sated wantons' (Houghton, 1957, p. 368). But Swinburne was an unsurpassably ardent fan of *As You Like It* too, writing himself, in fact, in the sublimated tones of so many other critics, as we shall see. Thomas Arnold had already condemned the comedies earlier in *The Christian Life* (1845), and his son Matthew, more liberal certainly, always held back something, some demarcated area of reserve, from fullest praise of the top names. Although Matthew doesn't mention *As You Like It* by name, the passages on Shakespeare in his renowned Preface of 1853 point hard at it.

Of a major poem, asks Arnold, 'What are the eternal objects of poetry, among all nations and at all times? They are actions; human actions; possessing an inherent interest in themselves'. Arnold then picks on Shakespeare himself. The playwright had every gift, but also 'a special one of his own; a gift, namely, of happy, abundant and ingenious expression, eminent and unrivalled . . . here has been the mischief'. (How exactly the view presages that of Terry Eagleton (1986), of

Shakespeare's single characteristic, 'extraordinary eloquence'!)
Reading Shakespeare's current imitators 'one is perpetually
reminded of that terrible sentence on a modern French poet – *il
dit tout ce qu'il veut, mais malheureusement il n'a rien à dire.*'
In English: he speaks just as he likes, yet sadly has nothing to
say.

'Just as he likes'; 'as you like it'; can a play with such a title
say much, did Arnold wonder? Is the title of his second chapter
in *Culture And Anarchy* (1869), 'Doing As One Likes',
knowingly a sort of word-level anagram of 'As You Like It',
a play Arnold himself had burlesqued at Oxford when an
undergraduate there? *Culture And Anarchy* itself appeared in
1869, the same disapproving '60s. That 'high seriousness'
meant the histories and tragedies is markedly exemplified by
the young Edward Dowden, later Professor of English at
Trinity College, Dublin, but publishing his book on Shakespeare – or 'Shakspere' as he always wrote – in 1875; that is to
say, only a few years after these rather discouraging events
occurred. (Incidentally Helena Faucit did Rosalind at Drury
Lane, yet again, in the same year. She was 58.) Dowden has eight
chapters. Only the seventh refers to the comedies at all. It
begins: 'A study of Shakspere which fails to take account of
Shakspere's humour must remain essentially incomplete.' It is
a touch concessionary, one feels, and *As You Like It*, and
indeed the comedies generally, are not fully covered. Yet
Dowden does usefully touch on the theme of melancholy, both
in Jaques and through the play more generally. He cites a
recent view of the play as 'an early attempt by the poet to
control the dark spirit of melancholy by "thinking it away"'.
And yet 'no real adversity comes to any of [the characters]. . . .
Of real melancholy there is none in the play.' 'It is the sweetest
and happiest of Shakspere's comedies. No one suffers.' Again,
two critical questions are raised: whether the play does somehow rebound from the sonnets, and whether the play has evil.
Dowden links the melancholic to the insubstantial and is only
one of many to begin to see Jaques as precursor to Hamlet.

Productions continued, of course. We have mentioned
some, but not yet the most famous, that of Charles Macready
back in 1841–2. Macready emphasised two things: an accurate
text at last, and elaborate stage-settings. Macready brought

back traditionally omitted passages and got rid of the lumber of imports, including *Love's Labour's Lost*'s Cuckoo Song with its albeit interesting cuckoldian implications. Agnes Lathem (1975) called this 'a very carefully considered production' for which we can in hindsight be grateful. But the stage-sets pushed Ardenism to its limits. Reynolds (1988, pp. 102–3) gives us the report of the critic from *The Spectator*, who was present. 'The sylvan scenes have a wild and primitive aspect... old trees of giant growth spread their gnarled and knotted arms, forming a "shade of melancholy boughs"' – (that phrase again) – 'for the banished Duke and his sylvan court; the swift brook brawls along its pebbly bed; the sheep-bells "drowsy tinkling"' – (Gray, not Shakespeare) – 'is heard from the fold on the hillside; and the lodge in the wilderness, overgrown with creeping plants, is musical with birds... the last scene, a stately vista of lofty trees, in which a floral temple is erected by the foresters to Hymen's altar, is a pretty fancy in pastoral taste.'

One might as well go outside; which is just what the players did at Coombe House, Kingston upon Thames, in June 1885, watched by, among others, Oscar Wilde. Jaques was played by Herman Vezin, who had been in the 1864 Bath production. On the 'outdoor' aspect Wilde's comments are astute. Tragedy can't be outdoor, for 'nature thinks nothing of disturbing a hero by a hollybush' (Salgado, 1975, pp. 161–8). In comedy it doesn't matter. An opposite view was taken recently by Robert Ornstein, an American critic, of the BBC TV production: 'the charm of Arden vanishes' as the actors 'pick their way through real underbush' and 'the Duke's banquet beneath melancholy boughs becomes as mundane as a family outing' (1986, p. 144). To Wilde, Phebe however is a 'Chelsea Chinese shepherdess' and her dress 'a panegyric on a pansy', and Rosalind's own dress 'absolutely displeasing'.

Indeed Wilde says much on clothing, and some disarmingly different remarks are included. Rosalind suffered much, we are told, 'through the omission of the first act', so that 'we saw more of the saucy boy than the noble girl'. More remarkable still perhaps is 'Lady Archibald Campbell's Orlando', for whom the wrestling scene brought out 'a possible absence of robustness in her performance'. No women's international rugby union yet, then, but the intriguing notion of two males (Orlando and Ganymede) played by two females, an eventuality of course to recur in the multitudinous girls' school-and-college productions of the early twentieth century. However, it is Wilde's own possibly fetishistic focus of interest that matters here. The *fin de siècle* is approaching, Lord Alfred Douglas has now 'rearranged' Shakespeare's sonnets, and the poet Algernon Charles Swinburne, already mentioned, has by now produced his own study of Shakespeare's work.

Swinburne takes camp to the outermost. After fifteen close pages of discussing whether Shakespeare authored *Arden of Faversham* (Swinburne doesn't remark the name) he comes to the comedies thus:

> At the entrance of the heavenly quadrilateral, or under the rising dawn of the four fixed stars which compose our Northern Cross among the constellations of dramatic romance hung high in the highest air of poetry, we may well pause for very dread of our own delight, lest unawares we break into mere babble of childish rapture and infantile thanksgiving for such light vouchsafed even to our 'settentrional vedoro sito' that even at the dawn out of the first depths *Goder pareva il ciel di lor fiamelle.* (Swinburne, 1880, p. 148. The 'heavenly quadrilateral' is the three mature comedies plus *A Midsummer Night's Dream.*)

The need to sublimate one's inner unmentionables continues; the increasingly intriguing question, for both sexes, is whether it is this very play *As You Like It* that arouses them.

To be fair, Swinburne also makes critical points. In *As You Like It* we never feel 'anything more lurid or less lovely than "a light of laughing flowers"' and 'we hardly feel . . . the presence or the existence of Oliver and Duke Frederick'. This last absence-of-evil point, if true, is deeply pertinent to the play's effect, as will be discussed later. Yet the context suggests bardolatry. Swinburne's one criticism takes him an apologetic seven lines:

> Nor can it be well worth any man's while to say or to hear for the thousandth time that *As You Like It* would be one of

those works which prove, as Landor said long since, the falsehood of the stale axiom that no work of man's can be perfect, were it not for that one unlucky slip of the brush which has left so ugly a little smear in one corner of the canvas as the betrothal of Oliver to Celia. (pp. 151–2)

Got it? The Oliver–Celia love-match is unconvincing. Again the Jaques-for-Celia tradition briefly surfaces. Swinburne was taken to task for this sort of thing by the poet Edward Thomas, who comments:

When [Swinburne] says that *As You Like It* is 'one of the most flawless examples of poetic and romantic drama . . . that ever cast its charm upon eternity' those last seven words are of no use except that they lengthen the sentence and make it more high-flown. The style suggests nothing but the sonorous lips of the rhetorician; it falls without an echo into the brain. (Thomas, 1981, pp. 146–7)

Why then do they all do it? Why does *As You Like It* so generate this need to say nothing-at-all? Here at once is another, only three years later: Edmund Gosse, writing about the forest in both this play and its precursor by Thomas Lodge (on whom he was an authority), then suddenly leaps into effusion on both: 'The light which is blown down the deep glades of Arden, and falls lovingly on the groups in this pastoral masquerade, is that which never shone on sea or land, but which has coloured the romantic vision of dreamers since the world began' (1883, p. 19). No doubt. The century ends with one of the great Rosalinds, Ada Rehan at the Grand Theatre Islington in 1897, reviewed approvingly indeed by Bernard Shaw: but he too, by now, has had enough. Ada Rehan, gifted to be sure, is too romantic and extreme, Orlando is 'a walking tribute to [the producer's] taste in tights', and Amiens, bearing winter and rough weather 'in a pair of crimson plush breeches, is a spectacle to benumb the mind and obscure the passions' (Salgado, 1975, pp. 161–8). On clothes, the comments of Shaw and Wilde alone add up to more than all previous critics put together. But again, this perceptive critic at least tries for a reason. 'Rosalind is not a complete human being: she is simply an extension into five acts of the most affectionate, fortunate, delightful five minutes in the life of a charming woman.' The feminists will hardly agree, but at least a new angle is placed on Mrs Jameson's self-knowing objection to elucidating Rosalind at all.

With certain incidental additions, the twentieth century down to about 1945 continues in the same vein. Surprisingly, the normally witty Dowden (1911, p. 667) maintained:

> [Shakespeare – or Shakspere] has written no happier play than this which tells of the love of Orlando and Rosalind, at once so earnest and sportive, as it moves through the sun-dappled spaces and over the dewy sward below the oaks of Arden. Arcady and England meet in this forest of France with its exotic fauna and flora. The genuine English peasant, the Dresden-China shepherdess, and the noble youth and maiden of romance cross each other in the greenwood.

In 1925 E.K. Chambers wrote that

> the temper of the play is so perfect, its poetry so mellow and so golden, that the critic would fain hold his hand in fear that, when all has been said, he shall but seem in his curiosity to have rubbed off the marvellous dust from the wings of a butterfly . . . we have nothing to do but to listen to the bugles blown as he hunts the quarry of his theme through the intricate glades and tangles of his bosky imagination. (p. 155)

Then 1926 brings Sir Arthur Quiller-Couch, introducing the Cambridge edition with Dover Wilson: 'he who knows Arden has looked into the heart of England and heard the birds sing in the green midmost of a moated island'. The play is incomprehensible to Continentals, especially Germans, who illustrate their non-understanding by actually disagreeing with each other. Quiller-Couch does usefully point out that 'Orlando' echoes 'Sir Rowland' (his father), and that only Orlando gets to Arden without getting tired.

The most useful gloss I have found on all this in pre-modern criticism had already come from Sir Walter Ralegh, an early

Professor of English at Oxford and whose book *Shakespeare* appeared in 1907.

> The best instance of the alliance of poetry with drama is to be found in *As You Like It*. The scene is laid, for the most part, in the forest of Arden. Yet a minute examination of the play has given a curious result. No single bird, or insect, or flower, is mentioned by name. The words 'flower' and 'leaf' do not occur. The oak is the only tree. For animals, there are the deer, one lioness, and one green and gilded snake. The season is not easy to determine: perhaps it is summer; we hear only of the biting cold and the wintry wind.

Ralegh's reason is theatre itself. 'So Shakespeare attains his end without the bathos of an allusion to the soft green grass, which must needs have been represented by the boards of the theatre' (Ralegh, 1907, pp. 126–7). Aside from the trivial point that Ralegh didn't count holly or olive as trees, one's reaction is simply: at last! But, unless the preceding writers were idiots, we must still ask why they wrote as they did. Not dwelling here on the point, let's simply draw up a checklist of possibilities:

1. Rosalind has no character, nor much the others.
2. The forest is allegorical.
3. Sex, transvestite or otherwise, can't be discussed.
4. Victorian fustian.
5. Bardolatry.
6. The lack of a framework of comedy criticism.
7. They were all dead right. The play is largely atmospheric; there is little more to add; yet we love it, so must say something.

In the early twentieth century the play continues to be produced, by professionals but increasingly by amateurs too. The rise of education for women and girls opens up many opportunities. The play appeared in London in 1907, 1911, 1929 (with Ralph Richardson as Orlando; in 1921, aged 18, he had played Oliver with a touring company) and twice in 1936. One of these last included Edith Evans as 'A Rosalind of calculated and enchanting mannerisms' (Lathem, 1975, p. lxxxix).

The eminent American producer Arthur Colby Sprague lists a 1941 production of *As You Like It* in New York as one of the four worst Shakespeare productions he ever saw. Another rather later New York production, by Michael Benthall in 1950, 'elaborated the pictorial' to the same extent as 'the aberrations of Augustin Daly' (the producer excoriated by Shaw earlier). Cuts and interlopations – the Cuckoo Song again – were an annoyance, as were the exiled Duke and his followers 'launching arrows at an unseen and certainly un-harmed stag' (1954, p. 161). The swooning scene ended with Oliver and Celia making love and 'Oliver's carrying Celia off in his arms'. The same old problems: how to infuse action, whip up the music, fix up Oliver–Celia, capture the elusive forest. It is interesting that Sprague found a better production elsewhere 'before plain curtains', for 'the words themselves create atmosphere when atmosphere is wanted'.

The women, sporadically, go on writing. Agnes Mure Mackenzie's book *The Women In Shakespeare's Plays* appeared in 1924. Her long subtitle is 'A Critical Study from the Dramatic and the Psychological Points of View and in Relation to the Development of Shakespeare's Art', and she begins: 'The whole play is simply the personality and fortunes of the heroine.' Yet a curious cop-out follows on Rosalind from our psychologist. 'There is not very much to say about Rosalind by way of analysis. She is intensely alive.' A rough-and-ready summary of sorts is, however, provided. Like Portia, Rosalind has a forthright outlook on the world and on conduct, gay humour and clear-sighted wit, and is a generous and whole-hearted lover. Mackenzie then traces the play through, much as Faucit did and Juliet Stevenson will later, interposing her own intentionalities into the 'Rosalind' who now has an inner self behind the script-lines. Rosalind 'pretends immense surprise' at Orlando's tree-poems, 'drops pretences in a hurry' on hearing he is near and 'takes imperturbably' his lateness from dinner. Celia is 'aghast', 'furious' at her father's conduct. Often, not always, textual evidence is given in support. The play's inaction is also underlined. '[The play has an] easygoing-ness of structure – in fact there is nothing, properly speaking, to construct. [Shakespeare] projects a group of people and uses them as the vehicle for vivid and entertaining talk, and that is all, or nearly so' (pp. 111–12, 117).

Virginia Woolf's novel *Orlando* (1928) is about an Elizabethan time-traveller who changes sex. Woolf could hardly have titled a novel with a character from Shakespeare's chief play on sex-disguise without even noticing; and she did, more than once, affirm her belief in the value of the 'androgynous mind' and that Shakespeare supremely embodied it. Beyond that, one can deduce little. James Joyce's *Ulysses* had appeared in 1922. The remarkable ninth chapter, a debate in a Dublin library, sees banishment as the heart theme of the whole Shakespearian corpus, particularly alluding to *As You Like It*, with its double-banishment, as unique.

In 1926 comes the Cambridge University Press edition of the play, edited by John Dover Wilson and Sir Arthur Quiller-Couch. The interest of Wilson's part of their Introduction lies in his dating of the play, already noted. Wilson points to 'verse-fossils' among the prose passages, and internal name and time contradictions; both of these suggest a play that has been revised. Lathem takes issue with this and concludes 1599, although she doesn't deny that it may have been based on an earlier, perhaps much shorter and privately performed, version. The *Scrutiny* critic James Smith published an essay on the play in 1940 (collected with other essays in 1974). Smith's emphasis is on the play's inaction, and Jaques as ur-Hamlet. In 1938 H.B. Charlton produced the first full book on Shakespearian comedy. It is, admittedly, rather disregarded now. We are happy with these characters rather than laughing at them: they aim not to preserve good but to enlarge it; and they do this finally, in the mature comedies, by enticing us into a larger wisdom by the imagination as that is brought out by a desire for delight. This process discovers the dominant heroine. She has mother-wit, common sense, affection given and received, competence for her ends, open-eyed lack of sentiment, modesty and awareness of others. The worst sin is ingratitude, as Amiens's song declares. It is not, however, just the Arcadia the poet traditionally longs for. In *As You Like It* the winter wind blows in the forest, and there is at least one malcontent in each play. There is magic, music and the fun of the gross body, though this last is less evident in *As You Like It* than elsewhere. Charlton at least set an agenda, even if it was to be discarded in the spate of comedy theory that grew up in its wake.

In the past forty years, in effect from the Second World War up to the present moment, theory and criticism of Shakespearian comedy, and of *As You Like It*, has reached a fully fledged professionalism. This has really grown out of two movements: first, the pioneering work of Charlton himself, L.G. Salingar and Northrop Frye, and the spate of studies from roughly 1950 to 1970 which followed; second, the corpus of feminist studies published since the 1960s. Rather than summarise these here I prefer to treat them as present material to be used directly in our own discussion forthcoming. As to the literary legacy, there is much pervasive, little specific, although some of Auden's poems betoken his interest in Shakespearian comedy generally, but also its green and classical background. The play seems to hover round 'Et In Arcadia Ego', 'The Truest Poetry is the Most Feigning' and 'Reflections In A Forest'. It remains only to name a few of the hundreds of productions of the play that have occurred in this last post-war period.

If the play does indeed lack action, evil and even character – *if* it does – yet if we still love it and want to see it, then, as Lathem says, in production at least it 'needs something to strive against' (1975, p. xc). The psychological and technological professionalism of the post-war period has enabled this. One of the first responses came with Vanessa Redgrave's Rosalind in 1962 and Dorothy Tutin's in 1967, courageous waif and boisterous tomboy respectively. Doubtless interesting Touchstones were Colin Blakely and Roy Kinnear. In 1973 Eileen Atkins did 'a Rosalind in jeans' (then still a novelty) with Richard Pasco as Jaques, a role he was later to repeat in the BBC TV production. For some critics of the Redgrave performance, incidentally, Rosalind the Heavenly was still with us:

> [she] snatches off her cap so that her hair tumbles like a flock of goldfinches into sunshine . . . [she] is a creature of fire and light, her voice a golden gate opening on lapis-lazuli hinges,

her body a slender supple reed rippling in the breeze of her love. (J.W. Lambert and Bernard Levin respectively, quoted in Reynolds, 1988, p. 91)

Perhaps she always will be.

Remarkable after 1965 is the variety of interpretations and stagings which appeared. Perhaps, again, the play's title invites it. In 1967 came the all-male production at the National Theatre. It seems to have provoked a row beforehand between John Dexter (NT Director) and Laurence Olivier, the latter fearing that Dexter was 'indulging himself in a drag show'. However, the production was broadly successful, odd though it is to think of the now middle-aged Ronald Pickup and Charles Kay as the lead females. The performance gave 'not the slightest offence' (*The Stage*), its aim being both spirituality and relevance. In 1977 there occurred an outdoor performance in Berlin-Spandau in West Germany. This apparently went to every length of ingenuity one could wish for or dislike. The audience had a fifteen-minute walk from court to forest after Act I, past a bear and a sleeping hermaphrodite and aided by airs from a following wind-machine. The forest contained trees, pond, waving cornfields, birds, singing shepherds, unromantic peasants' hovels, and botanic and zoological collections. A large, partly unfolded globe stood in the acting area. Rosalind *et al.* arrived with a cart like refugees. The deer was skinned by its captors on stage, as in 1879. Jaques was dressed variously as magician and/or witch; Robin Hood, Robinson Crusoe and sundry twentieth-century philosophers sporadically appeared; and Phebe wept uncontrollably at the end, to the end. The acting, it seems, was very good, the love scenes tender and lyrical. In 1986 at the University of California, Santa Cruz, there was also an outdoor perform-ance, less ambitious. The audience's walk was only fifty yards. The production was notable for a Hymen silently appearing as invisible watcher of the scenes between the lovers, sitting on an arch, or in the crook of a tree.

Film and TV are themselves outdoor by the nature of the case. In 1935 Laurence Olivier had played Orlando in a filmed version, being trained by professional wrestlers for the pur-pose. But the camera cannot lie: Olivier could not make his failure to recognise Ganymede believable. The BBC TV version has already been alluded to. It is inevitably somewhat 'educational' and the more vigorous scenes, the wrestling notably, are unconvincing in the extreme; yet to this viewer the close-up technique of TV made the love scenes ravishing. Here the non-recognition *was* believable, for Rosalind at court has a painted, ghostly white face and formal Elizabethan wide dress to the ground, while in the forest her hair is curly, her face fresh and her breeches like comfortable Oxfam trousers. Brian Stirner played opposite Helen Mirren. A new film version is to be released this year (1992) with Emma Croft as Rosalind.

Two dream-mirror versions were the Adrian Noble RSC production in 1986 and an Edinburgh Festival production in the same year. On his largely surrealist set, Noble had Jaques early on walk through a standing mirror into Arden and back through it again, presumably to reality, near the end. The Edinburgh producer had Rosalind and her yuppie friends go for a picnic right at the start; Rosalind lies down on a bank, goes to sleep and dreams the entire play. (At the Tragic Theatre, Washington, in 1977, the 'sequester'd stag' scene was also a dream of Rosalind's.) These versions of course recall Lewis Carroll. In the first draft of *Alice* Carroll called Alice 'Lacie', an anagram of course of that name (Hudson, 1954, p. 144). But Alice also anagrams 'Celia', and many intriguing thoughts are provoked. Carroll was indeed referring to Alice Liddell, for whom and whose sisters he wrote the story, but he liked anagrams, liked Shakespeare, and wrote in the disapproving 1860s to which we have referred. Such stuff are dreams made on.

Three recent actors have left accounts of productions in which they played. Simon Callow played Orlando for John Dexter's National Theatre production in the late 1970s. Dexter it seems was a domineering and physical director, who 'decried all previous productions of the play as lyrical and mellow, whereas it was, initially at least, harsh and tragic' (1985, p. 108). Dexter saw the love scenes as really teaching scenes (he hasn't been alone in that emphasis) and the play's basic theme as ingratitude. Callow felt the production offered 'no release of joy, no sense of the culminating harmony which is the destination of every Shakespeare comedy' (p. 112). John Bowe

played the same part in Terry Hands's RSC production of
1980. Bowe's account (Brockbank, 1985) is gentle and humorous, in the play's spirit; he recalls particularly the wrestling in
which he was flung – intentionally – into the front row of
the audience, but on one night broke a shoulder-blade. The
wrestling emphasis demonstrates the need of directors to fill in
with theatrically powerful effects. Bowe also thought Rosalind
'plays cruelly on Orlando's emotions', so that again two versions of Rosalind become available, this time in the same
experience. In this production Jaques attempted to seduce
Rosalind (presumably IV, i, 1–24), an interesting variant on the
traditional Jaques–Celia urges. Juliet Stevenson was Rosalind
in Adrian Noble's production of 1986. She makes many
absorbing comments, such as that early on Rosalind 'often
leaves a thought uncompleted', evolving from them to the
'extraordinary arcs of thought' in those long, rippling sentences in the later acts. But Stevenson imputes to Rosalind any
amount of feelings, reactions, emotions and purposes which,
quite simply, can be read differently and as the play's title
invites. As we have seen, the question whether Rosalind is a full
character or a set of words runs long through *As You Like It*
criticism.

I saw the Adrian Noble production of 1986, the 1990 RSC
production of John Caird and, in the same year, a university
production in the Burton-Taylor rooms at Oxford. All three
fought mightily to escape the Macready–Faucit straightfor-
wardness, always a challenge when as-you-want-itness is an
ever-present temptation to go to superfluous theatrical lengths.
Stevenson lay voluptuously on her back before an Orlando
almost wholly incredulous, but a main feature for this spectator was the outstanding Jaques from Alan Rickman, he of
Obadiah Slope fame in the TV version of Trollope (since then
Rickman and Stevenson have also played opposite leads in the
film *Truly, Madly, Deeply*). This Jaques was an overweight
lout, body too big for his itchingly whingeing though finally
unmalicious mind. Not all reviewers liked the production,
feeling the surreal scenery made the court–countryside distinction disappear altogether. The John Caird production had a
massive, stark, black, rectangular stage set throughout, back-
cloth to deathly ballroom dancing in the court scenes, and for

huge jungle trees in the forest. Stunning weather effects were dynamically achieved: fog and mist, fluttering autumn leaves from sixty feet up and then falling snow, and a summer made of butterflies in the air and a vertical overhead spotlight. Celia's predicament grew more painful by the scene and Rosalind's faint revealed a hitherto concealed near-neurotic disturbance. Stealing the show perhaps was Mark Williams's Touchstone. He wore black tie with no jacket and red hair in a crew-cut. With Comic Relief nose later thrown disgustedly on the floor he became for all the world a Steve 'Interesting' Davis parody, so that the Seventh Cause speeches came gesturally to life in a way their late interpolation doesn't often allow. At Oxford the students produced an ingenious special effect for every scene, a languorous female Jaques, a Prince-Charles Duke Senior, a wimpish bespectacled Orlando, a commandingly vicious Oliver, a mafia-looking Duke Frederick, a weak-at- the-knees Adam and a bossy likeable Rosalind. Rosalind hurled herself physically on top of Orlando and the poor lad had no chance.

Without wishing to sound easily impressed I would say all three productions were successful, in that all the many themes we have seen picked up gradually over the last three centuries – the absence of action, the character-not-character of Rosalind, the feel of the outdoor, the balanced melancholy of Jaques and generally, the 'sprightly dialogue' and interactive relationships, the Oliver–Celia problem, the under-the-tree theme, the unspoken sex and its adjacent clothing, and the endless enchantment of love – fade into and out of all these post-war productions as possibilities that always hover, never wholly confirmed. Finally, it is no small thrill to be able to record that, even as I write, three more London productions are in prospect for this summer of 1992 (with Samantha Bond, Jemma Redgrave and Cathryn Harrison as the respective Rosalinds); and that only last year saw an all-male *As You Like It* put on with notable success by the Cheek By Jowl company at the Lyric Theatre, Hammersmith. Adrian Lester, the male Rosalind, has recorded the difficulty but great interest of playing the various Rosalind–Ganymede complexities, himself a man. In the last analysis our much-loved play does indeed perhaps 'need something to strive against', in the vigour of production if not in the solitary reading to which we inevitably return, and to which we turn now.

· I ·

Non-action

The play is built on an atmospheric basis of talk and tactics, philandering and philosophy, ardour and Arden. The 'action' of reversal, dilemma and conflict, seen as the basis of drama since Aristotle, is knowingly missing. The political-power of the play's opening fades tamely away before a gradual soft foliage of love-power always before our eyes, and the play's firmer core turns out to be the 'wooing scenes', as they are usually known, in Acts III and IV. In between, Act II has been stolen by the solitary Jaques alone.

There is no military or political conflict at all. No motive is given for the usurpation of the throne now held by Duke Frederick, so Duke Senior is given no motive for a recapture other than the general human one we may broadly infer. And he and Orlando never so much as hint at a plan of recapture. This is the more marked in that, differently from the Old Comedies of the tradition, there is no rivalry between these two; the usual father-in-law/son-in-law tension (not that Orlando is yet married) does not exist. Indeed, it is positively denied in Act II where Duke Senior states, 'If that you were the good Sir Rowland's son/. . . Be truly welcome hither. I am the duke/ That lov'd your father' (II, vii, 194, 198–9). In short, there would have been nothing to hinder any military recapture co-operation if that had been wanted. Furthermore Orlando's interruption of the banquet could have led to a dramatic quarrel; rather, it led to a gracious forbearance by the Duke and Orlando's admission of his own mistake and his gentle reply. Duke Frederick himself gives no reason for hating Sir Rowland; 'I did find him still mine enemy' is the last word on the subject. If we feel urge to know why, it is for personal not political reasons, for no political question presses.

Nor are there any important love rivalries. Of the two that do occur, Phebe's for Ganymede is abortive from the outset as the audience always knows, and Touchstone's curt dismissal of William as late as Act v is over as soon as introduced. Rather, we are led into a compelling mix of melancholy and delight by a love affair in which, however, the lovers themselves effectively never fully meet, not because of any external barrier but one self-imposed, by Rosalind in that she opts to keep her disguise going even when she ceases to need it. And it would be difficult to think of this affair without its melancholic underpinning, for Rosalind's early sadness is compounded by the weighty presence of the 'melancholy Jaques' in the scenes between her depression and the developing love with Orlando.

Many have noted this non-action quality of the play before, but Harold Jenkins (1955) first gave sustained attention to its implications and details. Some post-war critics (e.g. McFarland, 1972; Felperin, 1970) doubted the completeness of this picture, with McFarland in particular suggesting that Shakespeare had to back-pedal fast to stop himself writing a tragedy. Felperin accepted the overall inaction view but excepted Orlando from it. But the surface action in Act I is also impotent in promise. That is to say, it is not merely inactive; there are also possible actions which come to nothing.

One might consider what Shakespeare could have done intead. Rosalind meets Orlando after the wrestling, not before. If he had lost there would have been no play. If she had met him beforehand, even more if she had known he was son of her father's friend, the wrestling bout would have been a dramatic turning-point with, if Orlando had lost, an issue to resolve, perhaps a tragic one. Equally Shakespeare could have set up the Orlando–Oliver fight with a kind of winner-takes-all formality. In fact this brothers' quarrel is little more than a wrangle, with an old man (Adam) watching with disapproving distress.

Even Lodge's balanced alliteration and gentle euphuism had more gut violence. Shakespeare took it out; most particularly by his omission of the whole ferocious story of how (in Lodge) Orlando and Adam escaped to the forest, killing about twenty of the Duke's men on the way; by the removal of the final battle when the Duke (Geriswood in Lodge) really does invade the forest; but also in the wrestling itself, where in Lodge the wrestler actually kills the two previous contenders. In Shakespeare, in that first act, any hint of dramatic conflict becomes inturned, somehow introspective. It has to be, for if it didn't we would always be distanced from the ensuing love-story by an anxiety, looking over our shoulders, as to what was still unresolved on a more political and violent level. But Orlando has no motive for his wrestling; there is no plot to avenge his father or become a hidden court insider. 'I come but in as others do, to try him with the strength of my youth.' Orlando's own self-abnegation follows (i, ii, 176–82).

The news of the previous bouts is unbloody and flat (115–22). We are drawn in further from the tingling our own nerves might have felt, by the deeper human questions the already established and thereafter ceaseless dialogue points to: Nature, Fortune, folly and wit, and love and melancholy itself. It is modified by the humorous (in the old sense as well as the modern; cf. Appendix B) teasing of the unsophisticated but good-natured Le Beau, and the repartee with Touchstone. The talk between Rosalind and Celia balances that between Orlando and Oliver not as competing possibilities for where the action will go, but as two pairs of emotional exchange. And no sooner does Oliver let out his savagery toward his brother than something defuses it: 'yet he's gentle, never schooled and yet learned'. And when in villainous plotting itself Oliver questions the wrestler about the overall court situation, we get, rather, a speech that sets the pattern of response for all that follows:

Oliver   Where will the old Duke live?
Charles   They say he is already in the Forest of Arden, and
    a many merry men with him; and there they live like the

old Robin Hood of England. They say many young
gentlemen flock to him every day, and fleet the time carelessly as they did in the golden world.

                                          (I, i, 114–19)

Arden

This liquid passage, and its wonderful last sentence, seems to
launch the play. The audience couldn't fail to have caught its
resonances and subliminal echoes, and have its own mood
settled and levelled in its witness of what then follows. And
Robin Hood was still popular. There had been two recent
Robin Hood plays in London of recent memory before *As You
Like It*. Our question then is how can this substitute for
drama's usual action, and the short answer is that Shakespeare's setting generates a number of fertile possibilities. This
fertility is literal: nature, trees, sheep, language and sexual love
all have growth potential which, when 'blocked' in Frye's term
for comedy's countermove – here by disguise – make for
situations, 'dramatic' or not, which interest us.

But the setting in this play is trees, the forest, the 'Forest of
Arden'. This is not only obvious, it is also formally declared,
three times: here as just quoted, and later when Celia makes her
saving proposal almost declamatory – 'To seek my uncle in the
Forest of Arden' – Act I's effective end. And when they arrive
there, Rosalind stops, and takes note of her new place: 'Well,
this is the Forest of Arden'. The audience, or some of them,
would have picked up the *et in Arcadia ego* echo in Touchstone's sardonic reply, and how he underlined place itself: 'Ay,
now am I in Arden, the more fool I; when I was at home I was
in a better place, but travellers must be content' (II, iv, 12–15).

'Arcadia' perhaps, but the scene is narrowly the forest, not
the full pastoral sweep. The shepherds and milkmaids (Corin,
William, Audrey), and the figures from traditional pastoral
romance (Silvius, Phebe) are the minor parts, as indeed are the
young men who 'flock' to the Duke. 'Silvius' is already thereby
named forester. There are shepherds but no shepherding or
sheep, and no cornfields; rather, we hear of oaks and acorns,
holly, olive, wood, trees and foresters themselves. But equally,
and despite the 'books in the running brooks', there is no

water. This seems deliberate. Lodge's 'John of Burdeaux' (John Seaboard) becomes 'Rowland de Boys' (Roland Woodman). There was, as it happens, a well-established de Boys family still living near Stratford in Shakespeare's time. Arden is warm and celestial, its 'winter fangs' a reference that disappears and was only there to hint at an adversity largely human. Furthermore when 'Nature' is discussed – as for example by Celia and Rosalind at I, ii, 39–54 – it is human nature, the 'nature' of John Lyly's then recent nature–nurture debate in *Euphues*. This nature could be moulded by humanistic learning into a rounded Renaissance man, but that debate's connection to vegetable nature is not made explicit by Shakespeare before the famous exchange between Perdita and Polixenes in *The Winter's Tale* (IV, iv, 76–103).

Arden, garden, Garden of Eden (and Adam), ardent, Mary Arden, Arden in Warwickshire, the Ardennes in France – there are many leads into what is suggested. Despite the frenchified names and the echo of the ardour of love, surely banishment away from political involvement and danger and onward to bliss are the most resonant impressions. Adam and Eve were banished from the Garden of Eden: our characters are banished to it. The myth is underlined by being reversed. They move from court and city out to the forest; back from the fallen world into Eden itself. The Eden theme seems to be tied to the pastoral theme as indeed Christianity itself is tied to pastoral through Virgil. The connecting symbol from that point of view is the under-a-tree theme, as I have put it, traceable back to the very first line of Virgil's *Eclogues*:

Tityrus, you lie shaded under your spreading beech tree, wooing the sylvan Muse on your thin pipe, while we leave our country and her sweet fields. We go banished, while Tityrus, in shady rest, tells the answering woods to name Amaryllis's beauty. (*Eclogue* I, 1–5)

As said earlier, with comic sexuality Celia finds Orlando 'under a tree like a dropped acorn'; Duke Senior and his followers live 'under the shade of melancholy boughs'; and Oliver is saved 'under an old oak, whose boughs were moss'd with age' by Orlando from a very Genesis-sounding serpent or

Old Testament lion. The tree has the Christian touch of crucifixion, and the sexual one of the phallus (Orlando seeming somehow to have shrunk to one of his own testicles), while the shade by which it is serviceable blocks out some of the sun and lets in a melancholic light. Along with this 'tree' is also the bush at points various, a female counterpart to the tree's phallus, and indeed, one feels, the forest itself. In the same forest a deer shoots across the clearing, is hit by an arrow or spear, and falls, writhing. Its silky sides pour down with sweat and blood.

Northrop Frye suggested that Shakespeare left the old comedy of Terence and Plautus behind him, evolving instead his own 'green world' drama from, in part, the holidays, festivals and spring rites of the medieval period and earlier. The emphasis turns from the agricultural productivity of sheep and corn to regeneration itself, winter cold, the greenness of spring, and love. *The Two Gentlemen of Verona, A Midsummer Night's Dream* and *The Merry Wives of Windsor* are seen as precursors, with, I would suggest, *Macbeth* as the crucial later case where evil equivocation of language comes in to warp the tree-world itself. If *As You Like It* does come from that tradition, it is because it is itself a holiday, for the playwright as much as for its characters, raher than depicting one, with God transposed into Jove and his fellows in the background. Meanwhile, despite the clearings of Saxon and Roman times, England's forests still covered four million acres in the sixteenth century (Hoskins, 1955, p. 139), with Arden alongside Epping, Dean, Sherwood and Wychwood as brand-leaders. To escape there did not mean tourism.

Trees talking

Rather, the trees do the talking – or at least are strongly and profoundly associated with it. Throughout *As You Like It* there is almost no place where trees are mentioned without clear naming close by of language itself, speech itself. In this most writerly of Shakespeare's plays, where the rippling surface of kinds of language most evokes fully human characters rather than their psychology or relationships first ordaining it, this language itself puts out shoots from the play's own generative powers, the forest and its associations. Descartes was soon to say that 'there exist no occult forces in stones or plants, no amazing and marvellous sympathies and antipathies' (in Easlea, 1980, p. 111); but he was speaking for the new mechanistic philosophy. However, since the main characters in *As You Like It* have been banished to the forest, rather than being native there, the trees do not speak, literally or allegoric-ally. Rather, language and speech join with the forest setting. But Ralegh's problem is perhaps answered here; one can't talk *about* the trees where the trees themselves are felt as the source of speech too. Duke Senior's quick reference to 'tongues in trees' carries more significance than he knows.

In Eden 'God spake'. In Arthurian legend sinister trees spelled like witches and the mandrake and its screaming root reappears in Donne. By the time of the Romantics nature is our teacher and the whispering aspens continue into the Georgian period. In this play it is perhaps counterpart to the 'babbling gossip of the air' in *Twelfth Night*. I count forty-one words, lines or places in *As You Like It* where there is reference to tree, forest, forester, oak, acorn, holly or some other wooded item. In every single case but one (see below) the reference stands right beside speech or language foregrounding its own nature even where there is a content-reference also. For anyone who wants to check them, here are the references for every case: Act I, i 41, i 114, iii 103; Act II, i 3, i 15, i 31, iii 63, iv 12–13, v 1ff., v 27–9, vi 6, vii 12, vii 111–16, vii 182 and 192; Act III, ii 5–6, ii 113, ii 124, ii 169–70, ii 173, ii 230–3, ii 255, ii 292–3, ii 295–6, ii 330 and 333, ii 350–2, ii 382, iii 38–9, iii 43–6, iii 58–9, iii 75, iv 29–30, v 73–5; Act IV, ii 5–6, iii 75–6, iii 97–121; Act V, i 22–4, iv 30–5, iv 40–2, iv 154–5, iv 169, iv 200–1.

Not surprisingly, these cases often arise from either Duke Senior's tongues-in-trees speech (II, i, 1–16), 'Finds tongues in trees, books in the running brooks,/Sermons in stones, and good in everything' (II, i, 15–16) or Orlando's curious reversal of that, in hanging verses back on the trees himself. By contrast Orlando's pinning of verses on to trees, as well as having his own passionate accompaniment at III, ii, 5–6, also occasions comments from others: 'Are you he that hangs the verses on the trees . . . ?' (III, ii, 381–2); 'I pray you mar no more trees with writing love-songs in their barks' (III, ii, 255–6);

'There is a man haunts the forest that abuses our young plants with carving "Rosalind" on their barks' (III, ii, 350–2). But the scope of these connections is wider. As said already, when the 'Forest of Arden' is mentioned it is declamatory, a formal announcement of intention to go there, or arrival there. In other places, including one of those, speech itself is named: '*They say* he is already in the Forest of Arden' (I, i, 114); 'who hath *promised* to meet me in this place of the forest' (III, iii, 38); 'Sir Oliver *Martext* . . . will you dispatch us here under this tree?' (III, iii, 58); '*Pray you*, if you know,/ Where in the purlieus of this forest stands . . . ?' (IV, iii, 75–6); 'Was't born i' th' forest here?/ Ay sir, I thank God/ "Thank God". *A good answer*' (V, i, 22–4) (italics all mine). The speech-reference may be reached through pun: 'Men of great worth resorted to this forest,/ *Address'd* a mighty power' (V, iv, 154–5). A clear alliteration may highlight it: '*First*, in this *forest*' (V, iv, 169). The speaker's way of speaking may be alluded to: 'here in the skirts of the forest . . . Your *accent* is something finer than you could purchase' (III, ii, 329, 333). Or its naming power noted: 'found him under a tree like a dropped acorn . . . It may well be *called* Jove's tree, when it drops such fruit' (III, ii, 230–3) (italics all mine).

Trees often occur in the songs, as in 'Under the greenwood tree' itself. But that then becomes explicit too: 'Well, I'll end the song . . . the Duke will drink under this tree' (II, v, 28–9); 'Have you no *song, forester*, for this purpose?' (IV, ii, 5–6). And a very powerful repetition may be an accompaniment: 'A fool, a fool! I met a fool i' th' forest,/ A motley fool' (II, vii, 12–13). Sheer utterance may be named: 'Then there is no true lover in the forest, else *sighing . . . and groaning* every hour' (III, ii, 297–8) (once again, my italics).

To be sure, in some places it is more tenuous than in others. Yet the single example from these forty-one where there is hardly any language-highlighting at all – Orlando's remark to Adam, 'But poor old man, thou prun'st a rotten tree' (II, iii, 63) – comes from Orlando himself, the one character who feels able to teach trees a thing or two about utterance by pinning his own verses on to *them*, and so reversing the word-current here indicated. Orlando's priority in this respect is marked in the nice bit of dialogue exactly where Rosalind first meets him:

Rosalind	Do you hear, forester?
Orlando	Very well. What *would* you?

(III, ii, 292–3)

– where Orlando misses, perhaps, his own woody pun. Orlando is not without wit, as is shown by his interchange with Jaques (III, ii, 249–89), but he takes time to get going and his remark is casual.

The tongues-in-trees motif seems to flow out through the play's lines as through tendrils or branches, and we are to understand a source of speech in them, even though the courtiers do not borrow direct but rather travel alongside. In his excellent study of the language of Shakespeare's comedies Keir Elam speaks comparably of a 'lingua adamica' which makes for 'not only a naturalizing of language but a linguisticizing of the natural scene' (1984, pp. 136–8). However, Elam gives perhaps too much weight to Orlando, whose role Elam says is to turn the landscape into a 'suitably figural poetic equivalent', reading the trees as they already are but also writing on their blankness. Elam thus suggests that nature needs the poet for its articulation, whereas surely in the play it is plain that Orlando cannot reverse the flow of material signification, which must have matter from which signs (whether spoken or written) can be made.

Where language itself is questioned in some way, trees drop away entirely. Jaques's 'all the world' speech, which emphasises the whining and complaining side of speech, has not one tree or forest reference. And Rosalind's run-down of male disloyalty in love at IV, i, 89ff. is about doing, not saying: it concludes briefly that 'these are all lies' and has no forest reference either. Orlando's protest to Oliver (I, i, 43–51) and Celia's declaration of love to Rosalind (I, ii, 7–13) have no explicit speech-reference nor forest-reference.

Richard Hooker wrote his *Laws of Ecclesiastical Polity* between the years 1593 and 1597, virtually contemporaneously, that is, with *As You Like It*. Hooker suggested that nature is one, though not the only, basis of law, in that law places all in proper order. But 'nature' and 'law' are already heavy abstractions which sit uneasily in talk about this play and its forest. Rather, as Hooker says, *natural law* is 'an infallible knowledge implanted' in the mind – what the trees say, we might put it – and neither human obedience to it nor mastery of it appear in Arden. They are one with it, and so it articulates.

Language

As is by now clear, the account so far is postponing what everyone will want to know: what the characters are, how they interact, what are their humours and moods, and how they love and declare and sacrifice themselves for love. True, and indeed, the advance of *As You Like It* from one of its clear precursors, *Love's Labour's Lost*, consists in the sense we have that it is ourselves, our sadness and joy, our tentative longings for another's warmth, our anger at a brother's injustice, our fear that our friend may betray us, that find their fullest expression in the later play. But it comes up from and seems wholly at one with its language. Portia's speeches in *The Merchant of Venice*, powerful as they are, seem more external to her; and the exchanges even as recently as in *Much Ado About Nothing* seem to install wit consciously into what is said. It is highly successful, but wit and articulation get separate attention there in a way *As You Like It* almost never needs. I have seen this play done many ways indeed, but the words never change.

As You Like It itself, its very first speech, begins with language's power to direct its own speakers strongly underlined. This then spreads out into wider, firmer forms, such as the songs, or the heavy and lengthy speeches given to Jaques. It turns from 'language' into 'talk', characters seem to grow before us, and the language has seeded interaction and a growing real-depth love, after the earlier love-at-first-sight conventional romantic love. The debates about poetry, but also truth and lies, are interspersed, and the play ends with certain language formalities, most notably Rosalind's and Silvius's formal spell-casting at v, ii, 51–122. This break-up of the play's parts into different types of writing, different weightings, pressures and powers, shows Shakespeare finally getting clear of the honeyed, constraining language of the Euphuists and Sidney's *Arcadia*, with their serene but elongated

elongated and wearisome movement to the right, an escape within which variation of human character, or even spoken presences, could not grow.

Two kinds of close verbal technique will have to suffice to illustrate these matters. One is alliteration, and the other is word-play or pun. The suggestion, always, is that somehow the forest, greenness, regeneration, life, are what enable them. The scientific mentality has not appeared; parts of a passage don't go back and question themselves, put in conditionals or jagged facts with no verbal essence and only formula. (It also seems to me – jumping the gun somewhat – androgynous, but that will be considered later.)

In almost the play's first words, Orlando complains about Oliver to Adam. 'His horses are bred better; for besides that they are fair with their feeding, they are taught their manage, and to that end riders dearly hired: but I, his brother, gain nothing under him but growth.' Orlando emphasises, but perhaps compounds, his frustration by matching one word with another, much as one leaf on a tree looks much like another yet is different. He soon has a chance to pitch this against Oliver, who returns it with equal competence. Later, early in Act II, Duke Senior has delivered himself of his strongly alliterative speech about the natural world. But soon afterwards the same word-matching is used jokingly by the Lord who recounts how he saw Jaques's self-dramatising sympathy with the stricken deer:

> . . . as he lay along
> Under an oak, whose antique root peeps out
> Upon the brook that brawls along this wood,
> To the which place a poor sequester'd stag,
> That from the hunter's aim had ta'en a hurt,
> Did come to languish; and indeed my lord . . .

Lay/along: an oak/antique: root/out: brook/brawls: place/poor: sequester'd/stag: from/aim: hunter/had ta'en/hurt: did/indeed: languish/lord – barely a physical detail or particle of thought escapes the elegant geometrical proportioning. But a moment later the Lord borrows with such accurate absurdity from the Anglo-Saxon kenning form – 'much marked of the melancholy Jaques' – that we have to ask what is controlling what, who whom. For a moment later the Lord seems to taunt Jaques with the same alliterative subjection, as though in Jaques (though not of course himself!) it is affected. He imputes to Jaques lines like 'that poor and broken bankrupt there . . . the body of country, city, court', and the rest. Elsewhere again, Adam gives Orlando a stark practical warning: 'this house is but a butchery./ Abhor it, fear it, do not enter it' (II, iii, 27–8), where along with but/ butchery there is butchery/abhor it, and the 'it' repeated.

Puns are a semantic alliteration. (I suggest later that they are transvestite.) We equally get 'two for one', but instead of two (or more) words sharing sounds, now two or more meanings do. *As You Like It* is littered with puns, though used with much tact by Shakespeare so that most take a second's notice and don't impede the human movement of what is said. They enrich humanly. At I, ii, 236, giving Orlando her chain, Rosalind calls herself 'out of suits with fortune', and the same word is punned much later during the closer wooing: 'Not out of your apparel, and yet out of your suit' (IV, i, 83); that is, Orlando's wooing itself. At II, i, 45, Jaques moralises his spectacle 'into a thousand similes', where I for one hear 'smiles' and Lyly's gently melancholic aim for euphuistic comedy: 'soft smiling not loud laughing', an echo at least some of Shakespeare's audience would have known. There are 'mounted' puns at III, ii, 88; 'horn' puns throughout; while at IV, i, 197 Rosalind's love 'cannot be sounded', when she has just spoken of the bottomless Bay of Portugal while trying also to express – sound – her love.

Underlying the whole play is another pun, never explicit but always there. It is a double pun furthermore: deer/hart – 'dear heart'; and one feels the tenderness provided by love, and needed by it, in the face of nature's most violent forces.

Talk and interaction

To the Elizabethans the world was not a randomly floating star-adjunct, with life on it the result of chance evolution. It was a created harmony, layered and ordered, with human placing a microcosmic equivalent to universal placing. The essence of rational consciousness lay in perception of analogies rather than processes. In such an atmosphere language, including everyday conversation, is used to elaborate such analogy rather than relate basically to others or just get things done. Language may parallel one's feelings, metaphorically and rhythmically, and be analogous to them; it will not merely point to them by variation of tone and body-language, or by explicit analysis of the speaker's feelings by himself or herself, as it is now.

Talk is the very medium of *As You Like It*. Action is absent, and language is abundantly rich, allegorical at least of the foliage of the forest where it occurs. The characters spend much of their time talking, simply talking. They change partners, and talk again. The modes of talk in the play are many. There are gentle and harsh exchanges. There are long speeches, as with Jaques most of the time, and shorter snatches. There is Touchstone's cabbagy prose (at III, iii, 42–57 almost reusing Falstaff's 'honour' speech from *Henry IV Part I*) and Phebe's terse, cat-like mouthings. There is Duke Senior's compact eloquent poetry about the primacy of nature, and Orlando's worse poetry claiming authority over it. There are lists of homogenous distributions – by Jaques and Rosalind severally near the end – and group chants where the characters seem to be under a joint spell, as when 'idle talking' is over. There are the elongating wistful curves by Rosalind where words multiply, and sharper comments from her companion Celia, who bangs home the same term sardonically five times as though she has had enough of it. There are long reportings of news (Oliver, de Boys), and shorter emergency ones as from Adam. There is the variation of rhythm and rise and fall between Orlando and Rosalind themselves, as for instance when she answers his four separate questions about time (III, ii, 300–27), as against the softer, more sinuous searchings back and forward as a little is withheld, a little revealed. There are Jaques's mournful dirges and there are the songs. The songs seem on a continuum with the rest rather than an unusual departure from an otherwise even-textured dialogue or prose.

In saying the play lacks action, what do we mean? What did we expect? The play eschews the events that usually mark comedy. There are no betrayals, love-elopements, ambushes, secret trysts, bed-tricks, night-time intrigues, about-turns, sleepings–wakings, intercepted letters, tell-tale gifts from unknown sources. When such things do occur – spells, mistaken identity, threats, eavesdroppings or give-away ornaments – they turn out somehow diluted, shadows of themselves; they affect nothing violently. No one actually mistakes anyone for anyone else. When any character eavesdrops, they then at once reveal themselves. Consequently the talk cannot arise from confrontation with real events. It is hypothetical, philosophical even; and even love, which is surely truly at the heart, is a compacting of the wider Renaissance 'delight' which Sidney sought in all poetic narrative.

The question again is of how character and language interrelate, and which dominates. Does character generate language, or language character? Each emphasis could be argued as typical of the Renaissance. The resulting growing implications of medieval science and of the humanism of Erasmus, Ascham and More – that we have minds and 'humours' and indeed 'parts', we are people, not merely reflections of God but microcosms of the world – would suggest that language was increasingly a product of those characteristics. Even the poet, maker with words, would have to follow Sidney's advice to himself: 'Fool . . . look in thy heart and write'. On the other hand the sixteenth century took great interest in rhetoric, the word 'in its very make-up, in its God-given or man-made origins, in its representational powers and in its social and ethical duties' (Elam, 1984, p. 22). This interest is evinced by among others Puttenham and Wilson. It suggests that the furthest one could get toward acknowledging the entity we today call 'interaction' was by using language as rhetoric, as language-intended-to-affect-others. For ourselves today, the quality of the words of daily interaction scarcely matter. What counts is that negotiation, as sociologists call it, is achieved, and the cultural practice of making relationships is accurately matched to the relevant personality or task context. But in Elizabethan England it was the drama itself which, by diversifying the modes of talk, perhaps found a way inward to an understanding of conceivably separated characters.

On that point, two things are striking. First, that Jaques's curiously detached speech about the stage (I think Shakespeare wrote it at a different time and worked it in, or wrote it specially for the Globe Theatre's opening) is none the less at the play's heart and is ambivalent. 'All the men and women merely players.' Where is the emphasis? If they are *merely* players, then language itself would seem to control them. But they must be players of men and women, and so at least those played must have separate selves – 'parts' now in another sense – so that even under the control of a created and hierarchical cosmos, at least they are people in that, not mere mouthings for speeches.

The other striking fact is that Shakespeare has entirely omitted Lodge's lengthy 'meditations'; that is, his characters' soliloquies. These are complex and often tortured in Lodge's *Rosalynde*; they contain wailings, self-tormentings, confessions and worries about what to do next. In *As You Like It* there is none of this. Yet Shakespeare is universally credited – justifiably, it seems to me – with creating more living characters in the play than Lodge did in the prose romance. This very fact is because Lodge, with the resources available to him, couldn't diversify the language enough for the reader to go through it into a sense that the characters have inner lives for which language merely serves as an expression.

We must not go to the other extreme, however. As Elam has said, to see the play as merely endless words exchanged, might be to 'fatally reduce the plays to a rarefied playing with rhetorical mirrors' (1984, p. 21). It would be too unreal to bear at all. It is rather that the characters – whether they generate language or it generates them – seem to have the leisure, in Arden, to try out what they feel/think/admire/enjoy/fear through language. All are slightly aware, if no more, that they and language are mutually interactive. In a brilliant article on conversation in this play Martha Ronk Lifson (1987) concludes that the play's 'Ifs' and 'Supposes' are the means by which a gentle deceit is used to further the details of love's attachment. By evoking such hypothetical matters on which the characters seem wistfully or cheerfully to ponder, we can enter their feelings, or 'their' feelings, even though we don't know them well as people. They are more like pleasant casual acquaintances, met in social life rather than working life. In the words of Francis Bacon, writing probably just about this time, 'discourse ought to be as a field, without coming home to any man' (1972, p. 103).

Bacon likened discourse to dance. 'The honourablest part of talk is to give the occasion; and again to moderate and pass to somewhat else; for then a man leads the dance' (1972, p. 102). And it was only the solitary Jaques who weighted the talk with his disputatious matter, and himself was 'not for dancing measures'. Montaigne (1958) too wrote about conversation. He said that nothing is more pleasurable than conversation. It is its manner, not its matter, that is important. The bane of conversation is the intervention of the learned and the logical, with their overweight knowledge and their tight systems. Shakespeare certainly read both, though whether he could have read the relevant Bacon essay by this time is uncertain.

Wrestling, hunting and sexual symbols

Yet all this talk of talk can still make for a certain evanescence. The play still needs some sense of gravity, some obdurate solidity of place which the shady and airy forest alone sketch in so ephemerally. In the first two acts there is a vigour in the wrestling and the stag-hunting themes which lasts in our memories later. They more than hint at sexuality too, although that is not their whole function. They serve to create physical events within the forest, which the forest itself never does, for there is no tree-feeling or planting, charcoal-burning, logging. These events then prevent the lightweight silky talk from taking off into the stratosphere.

The sense of a 'thingness' unique to each play occurs in most of Shakespeare. The sumptuousness of *Antony and Cleopatra* and the sea, storms and plants of the late plays are only two examples. In *Julius Caesar*, curiously and despite the early night-time omens and the later battle, it is people's faces, seen close up, reflected or cowled, that evoke the equivalent presence, suggest what is to be seen. The most overt dependence on objects occurred a little earlier, in *The Merchant of Venice*. In that play the story's attention is focused throughout on clear sets of objects: the caskets, the pound of flesh, and then the rings in Act v. Each has its own sex-or-violence connotation (Freud thought the caskets were wombs). From the moment Shylock and Antonio strike their chilling bargain in Act I, right through to the ring-joke's outcome in the play's very last scene, there is hardly an event or passage which is not concerned with which casket will be chosen, whether Antonio can be spared his bloody penalty, or whether Portia's and Nerissa's possession of their husbands' rings can be resolved. In *As You Like It*, with its endlessly abstracted encounters and discussions, an underpinning of the physical is not only equally necessary; it is the more certain to throw its own symbolic light over such verbal intercourse, for it is less than usually associated with 'plot' at a different dramatic level.

The wrestling bout of Orlando v. Charles is not described, not even by a line. But wrestling itself has already been primed up by Le Beau's long invitation to Rosalind and Celia to come and see it, and his vivid description of the previous bout, just finished. Touchstone's sardonic comment on this 'sport' makes the point: 'Thus men may grow wiser every day. It is the first time that ever I heard breaking of ribs was sport for ladies' (I, ii, 127–9). Even earlier, the interchange between Oliver and Charles the wrestler had alluded to breakage of limbs, neck and finger. After the wrestling the switch into a potentially sexual equivalent is immediate. Charles himself is borne quickly off-stage, but Orlando and Rosalind feel, it seems, that the bout had different import:

> Rosalind   Sir, you have wrestled well, and overthrown
> More than your enemies.
>
> (exit)
>
> Orlando   O poor Orlando, thou art overthrown!
> Or Charles, or something weaker masters thee.
> (I, ii, 244–5, 249–50)

In the next scene Rosalind's melancholy is not assuaged, and Celia knows why:

> Celia   Come, come, wrestle with thy affections.
> Rosalind   O they take the part of a better wrestler than myself.
>
> (I, iii, 20–1)

– with 'part' no doubt already getting a belly-laugh for the
proles in the pits. In immediately then trying to turn the 'jest'
into 'good earnest' Celia still can't resist the play on 'fall' as
common to wrestling and love. In the next scene we are in
Arden. Duke Senior's famous words about the sweetness of
adversity and tongues in trees and books in the running
brooks come at once, and take only seventeen lines. We
are then immediately presented with the taunting of Jaques
in his absence, but by means of a vivid, evocative, highly
physical description of the wounding of the 'poor sequester'd
stag':

> The wretched animal heav'd forth such groans
> That their discharge did stretch his leathern coat
> Almost to bursting, and the big round tears
> Cours'd one another down his innocent nose
> In piteous chase
>
> (II, i, 36–40)

The wrestling got no such description, but nor does any
person either, anywhere in the play. When discussing this
hunting and killing, critics often focus on the 'animal rights'
comment of Duke Senior at II, i, 22–5. But the actual evocation
of this picture is more moving still. It is beyond debate, and for
audience and reader equally mingles lastingly with other deep,
hidden urges and responses – sexual, violent and otherwise.
We recall it later when Rosalind says she 'will not kill a fly'
(IV, i, 106) and at Oliver's late conversion. This last, in context
of Orlando's rescue of him from the lioness, is again a reaction
against blood.

Of course, the hit is at Jaques himself, 'weeping and commenting upon the sobbing deer'. But it is achieved indirectly,
via the physical evocation of an animal, as though in this
play no physical person can be presented, so that any solid
description goes to evoke a mood or a personality. It is scarcely
possible to forget this broken stag later when horns themselves
weigh on Touchstone, Rosalind and Jaques severally. Touchstone fears marriage in Arden even more than anywhere else,
for 'here we have no temple but the wood, no assembly but
horn-beasts'. Yet he need not be ashamed, for 'the noblest deer

hath them as huge as the rascal', it is his wife's doing not his own, and it is better to be married (and cuckolded) than single. For 'by so much is a horn more precious than to want' (III, iii, 43–4, 50–1, 56–7) – a view whose cynical acceptance, incidentally, it is quite impossible later for the prouder and more truly noble Othello to share.

In teasing Orlando as she teaches him to woo, Rosalind widens this theme. For she says she would prefer to be wooed by a snail, whose slowness at least 'brings his destiny with him' – his horns – so that he is 'armed in his fortune, and prevents the slander of his wife' (IV, i, 54–5, 58–9). Jaques's own speech about the boy 'creeping like snail/ Unwillingly to school. And then the lover – ' has tacitly underlined this theme, hinting perhaps at boy-actors too. Certainly the Puritans such as Rainolds objected to boy-acting on such grounds. So the horn-song itself 'What shall he have that kill'd the deer?' – late on in Act IV – continues the play's necessary physical presence. Jaques, rarely for him, makes a practical suggestion: 'Let's present him to the Duke like a Roman conqueror; and it would do well to set the deer's horns upon his head for a branch of victory'. The ensuing song is rough, bawdy, clothes-orientated:

> His leather skin and horns to wear . . .
> Take thou no scorn to wear the horn . . .
>   Thy father's father wore it . . .
> The horn, the horn, the lusty horn . . .
>   (IV, ii, 11ff.)

The so-called 'victor' is ridiculously presented as the gull that, shoulder-high, he must seem to be.

There are also strong sexual symbols planted early, one each for Rosalind, Orlando and Celia. Rosalind's first moment of initiative occurs when disguise is suggested (Stevenson, 1988, p. 103). In detailing it, her first wish is for 'a gallant curtle-axe upon my thigh' (I, iii, 113), according to Freud the common locus for dream-displacement. Our 'penis-envy' is Montaigne's 'defect in sex' (Greenblatt, 1988, p. 66). But Rosalind has already put a chain round Orlando's neck, itself a sexually symbolic act. When they part he ruminates:

Can I not say, 'I thank you'? My better parts
Are all thrown down, and that which here stands up
Is but a quintain, a mere lifeless block.

(I, ii, 239–41)

The pun on 'quintain' as female pudenda would have been
picked up by the audience at once. Phallic erection, it seems, is
lost ('My better parts/ Are all thrown down') and replaced by
a feminine counterpart. 'Acquainted' comparably occurs later
from Jaques to Orlando at III, ii, 266–8: 'Have you not been
acquainted with goldsmiths' wives, and conned them out of
rings?' The pun connects to the chain Orlando is still wearing.
So here with 'quintain' the hint is that the virile Orlando may
also be androgynous, may share womanhood himself. Celia
conveys a different bodily anxiety. She will 'with a kind of
umber smirch my face' (I, iii, 107–9). Her need to hide herself
altogether was already clear at the wrestling: 'I would I were
invisible, to catch the strong fellow by the leg'. Celia's ambivalence as to whether (analytically speaking) she would couple
or castrate is the base-line in her attitude to 'strong fellows'
throughout.

Our emphasis here is general. In this early part of the play
there is a physical vigour, found in the wrestling, hunting, the
recurring horn symbol and the psychoanalytically loaded
objects just mentioned, such that a play so full of gracious talk
as this one can be anchored, not in eventful action, but in the
materiality which underlies our actions and indeed existences.
The wounded stag is behind the whole play: because it grounds
Jaques's melancholy, and that itself is silent modifier of the
wooing to follow.

So one can now talk about the characters in the play, or some
of them, with these first considerations in mind.

· 2 ·

Duke Frederick

At III, ii, 335ff. Rosalind has just met Orlando in the forest for the first time. She tells him: 'An old religious uncle of mine taught me to speak, who was in his youth an inland man, one that knew courtship too well, for there he fell in love. I have heard him read many lectures against it'. Who is this 'old religious uncle', who recurs elsewhere? Why, her uncle Duke Frederick, of course.

Some of the first post-war critics (Jenkins, 1967, p. 116; Hunter, 1962b, p. 32) saw Duke Frederick as simply a performer of evil by his usurpation and tyranny. Machiavelli had written earlier in the century and Shakespeare knew his work at least indirectly; for example, from *The Jew Of Malta*. But Duke Frederick is no Machiavelli, and indeed part of the non-action of *As You Like It* is the absence of any political manipulation in its story. Unlike Bolingbroke, Brutus or Coriolanus, Frederick is given no inclination for setting one faction against another, protectioneering, skill in troop recruitment or any other of the great man's devices. This absence leaves the Duke with only his own emotions regarding what he has done; his anxieties seem not political but familial. Radical critics now turn the picture upside-down and see Frederick and Oliver as heroically presuming to remove the established order which, of course, the bourgeois Stratford landowner restores at the end. Other critics (Leggatt, Ornstein, Berry) see him as more nearly vulnerable and uneasy. That seems nearer the mark, but Duke Frederick is surely not comedy's original *senex iratus* either. He has himself an embroilment in the action of which he is depicted as aware.

Shakespeare's interest in brother-quarrelling has been noted all along (Joyce, Rowse and others). Rowse (1976, p. 21) finds Shakespeare referring to the Cain–Abel story at least twenty-five times in his work, and in this Edenesque play it is more than usually pressing. We do not easily recognise it, because Shakespeare was, no doubt, suppressing any suggestion overtly that the usurper could be in the right and the old duke a pompous inept who should never have had the throne in the first place. But, even if Shakespeare was not of the devil's party without knowing it, he surely expresses a pattern of family relationship here which is always, one feels, behind or inter-woven with even his most overtly political plots. He can't make other than central Coriolanus's mother and wife, the Macbeths' strangely touching marriage, or indeed the curse of Queen Margaret on Richard III. The historian Alan Macfarlane, writing about the seventeenth-century diaries of a clergyman-farmer Ralph Josselin, says, 'I was startled to find . . . how "modern" his world was: his family life, attitudes to children, economic activities, and the very structure of his thought was very familiar indeed' (1978, p. 3). Frederick, like his brother, has no wife we ever hear of, nor 'economic anxieties', but his relations with his daughter and niece make up most of the story which comes through clearly now.

'The duke is humorous' (Le Beau at 1, ii, 256). By 1600 the word had begun to shift toward 'sardonic', 'jocular', while still retaining its medieval meaning too (see Appendix B). Jenkins (1967) suggested that the court 'stifles fun'. Certainly the humour may have gone sour, but it lies there, occasionally surfacing, in the Duke's words. He is, or was but still fleetingly is, capable of sensitivity to others, and aware of that good aspect in human relationships. On hearing that the youth before him is his enemy's son he says, after a brief startlement, 'But fare thee well, thou art a gallant youth – / I would thou

hadst told me of another father' (i, ii, 218–19). Indeed he had
already attempted to dissuade Orlando from the unpromising
wrestling encounter. He says at that point (i, ii, 148–51): 'In
pity of the challenger's youth, I would fain dissuade him, but
he will not be entreated. Speak to him ladies; see if you can
move him.' His words to the two ladies just before could be
sarcastic, but as easily affably jocular: 'How now daughter and
cousin? Are you crept hither to see the wrestling?' Most
delicious of all, his retort to Oliver:

> *Oliver*   O that your Highness knew my heart in this!
>   I never lov'd my brother in my life.
> *Duke F.*   More villain thou.
>
> (iii, i, 13–15)

Duke Frederick is hardly placed to remonstrate about lack of
brotherly love, but there is more to it, for we know of no love
in the opposite direction. Frederick says not a word against
either Sir Rowland or his own brother.

   This reading of his attitude to his niece may explain something
about herself as well as him. When he banishes her, it is just after
her apparent interest in the 'youth' the Duke himself has
admired. Well, if he the Duke were indeed this old religious
uncle who tried to dissuade Rosalind from love, what more
likely than that a spurt of love-jealousy should well up in him
at that moment – the very moment when she fell for the son of
his old enemy? He knew he was wrong; he knew their younger
affection was a new growth he should not envy. He could give
no reason: 'Thou art thy father's daughter, there's enough'. This
of course deceives nobody, for as Rosalind answers, 'So was I
when your Highness took his dukedom'. Frederick's neurotic
response is to shut her up and accuse *her* of pretending all
innocence and no traitorous behaviour. He calls Celia 'fool'
twice in his impatience, but unwittingly thereby may be suggesting a preference for the niece over the daughter:

>   she robs thee of thy name
> And thou wilt show more bright and seem more virtuous
> When she is gone.
>
> (i, iii, 76–8)

And when Celia says 'I cannot live out of her company' Duke Frederick's very abrupt reply suggests, underneath, 'neither can I'; i.e. I would sooner banish her myself than see her leave, to marry perhaps, of her own accord.

This must be why, the last time we see him, the Duke has become desperate to get Orlando back. He can't admit to wanting Rosalind herself back but that is what he wants. In so emphasising, he is – rather movingly – reversing his own decree of banishment. It is when a lord tells him that a nurse 'believes wherever they are gone/ That youth is surely in their company' that Duke Frederick sends for Oliver, Orlando's brother, to raise a search:

> Send to his brother. Fetch that gallant hither.
> If he be absent, bring his brother to me;
> I'll make him find him. Do this suddenly:
> And let not search and inquisition quail
> To bring again these foolish runaways.
>
> (II, ii, 17–21)

'Inquisition' sounds a chilling note, but there is still an echo of 'bring home safely' in the first three words of the last line. There is even a dying cadence down to 'these foolish runaways' (it could have been treacherous, villainous, wicked, etc.) from the man who, with mocking self-knowledge, called himself 'the better part made mercy'. Rosalind's attitude to 'fathers' (III, iv, 34) derives from her relationship with this uncle. He once loved her, told her stories, amused her with his evident wit and was himself 'religious' enough later to undergo conversion. When for whatever reason he turned sour, he focused on her with a jealousy which was not, however, incurable. As Celia said of his insistence that on her father's banishment Rosalind herself stay: 'It was your pleasure and your own remorse'.

Shakespeare probably only resolves the career-long brother-dilemma in *The Tempest*. The surrogate solution Orlando–Oliver here doesn't resolve it. Nor does the death of Claudius, for young Hamlet dies too; nor the death of Edmund in *Lear* – so clearly sequent to this play – for by that time the weight of emotional release has transferred to daughters and sisters. Prospero's 'magic' may be a sublimation of Frederick's.

Jaques

There have been marked differences in critics' interpretations of, and liking or disliking for, Jaques since criticism of the play began. Two of the more influential post-war women writers on the play differ on him entirely. Helen Gardner wrote him off wholly, as not joining in, 'preferring the pleasures of superiority' and 'liking himself as he is' (1959, p. 30), while Agnes Lathem (1975) would hear hardly a word against him. 'He is the very essence of sophistication . . . he has dignity and a sardonic charm . . . he breathes [Arden's] air easily and enjoys it. He flowers there' (p. lxxxvi–lxxxvii). It is hard to reconcile such positions.

It might then be best not to enter this character-preference debate but rather to see Jaques, likeable or not, where he is so important; that is, structurally. Structurally Jaques's position is clear. If Duke Frederick dominates Act I, then we might have expected, on reaching Arden, his brother to move centre stage in Act II. But in fact, as we have seen, Duke Senior does so only briefly; his leadership is nominal. It is Jaques who dominates Act II, replacing Frederick as the chief blocking factor and, in effect, blocking the development of Duke Senior also. This blocking occurs partly through Jaques's isolation. He converses with others, of course, but very much on his own terms. Strangely enough, this effect of isolation is actually increased by Jaques's express liking for Touchstone (II, vii, 12–43; V, iv, 103–4). By such interest and approval Jaques aligns himself with the play's other fool–intellectual presence and so avoids our being distracted by a duality at that point. His own solitariness is made more digestible.

But, as well as that, it is the length and single sweep of Jaques's speeches in Act II that make for this blocking effect. They delay and contrast the play's usual light-of-touch movement, for we are drawn in to their actual content as well as to what they say about their imagined speaker. Jaques's speeches, although among the play's longest, do not outstrip the rest on a line-count as much as they seem to by impression. Prelude to them has been the similarly long speeches, already discussed, *about* Jaques by the Lord who describes the hunting and the wounded deer. These speeches themselves have already slowed

down our response to a single character and made us ready to
weigh and savour him. Jaques then, in effect, dwells lengthily
and rather intensely on three things: the fool and his role; his
own right to speak to the world; that world itself as a mere
stage of stage players (II, vii, 12–61; 70–87; 139–66). Each
subject draws us, and we are forced to stop and look at each
along the play's road.

Again, it is the language that reveals the personal weighting.
In half-delightedly, half-sardonically applauding this clown he
has unexpectedly seen lying on the forest grass, Jaques uses
the word 'fool' (or 'fools' twice) seventeen times. 'Folly' and
'foolishly' bring it up to twenty. He has already said the word
five times in the first three lines, hammering it home with an
alliterative echo too: 'As I do live by food, I met a fool', as
though the two things could carry equal weighting in any sane
perspective on the world. It isn't entirely clear what Jaques
is saying he sees in Touchstone. It seems to be simply the
freedom that motley gives, no doubt along with praise for
Touchstone's hour-by-hour detachment in that role. This
speech, bar eight words from the Duke, lasts nearly fifty lines.
It ends with a sharp change of mood. 'Fool' becomes 'foul' –
Jaques will 'cleanse the foul body of th'infected world' (II, vii,
60) – just as 'food' became 'fool' at the start. This sudden
nastier taste comes with a newly expressed contrast between
foolish and wise (47, 53, 56), for Jaques's Erasmus-like praise
of folly is left ambiguous as to whether he attacks the wise or
feels wise himself.

Challenged then by the Duke he becomes defensive. He
says in effect that his castigations hurt no one so long as he
names none. But the loudness of his protestations is what grips
us, surely; it is this, still, which is drawing us to slow down
from the play's advance. For the play's conversational charm
depends on the opposite of Jaques's attitude. Partners to conversation's dance must work with the rhythm of the whole,
and even in hostility they must work point and counterpoint
into what they say, as for example did Orlando and Oliver at
I, i, 29–51.

This is not to fault someone called 'Jaques'. Again the matter
is structural. A counterweight to that light-of-touch talk is
needed; a contrast to a contrast. Rosalind was herself melan-

cholic at the play's start, and by having Jaques gather that grey matter into himself, into one isolated individual, Rosalind is freed for the wooing's later ease and spread. It liberates it, the very thing Jaques himself claims is desirable. As a result, the 'all the world's a stage' speech, most renowned of all Jaques's speeches, can be both weighty in content but now far less introverted, at once.

That last long speech of Jaques is, indeed, formal for that reason. That is not to say it feels merely insincere, rather that it becomes public property. The play is released by it, and also taught by it – not in drear didactic fashion, for the lovers (bar Orlando) don't even hear it. Rather, the *play's* weight of melancholy is gathered into Jaques and then discharged by him. It seems therefore to have a wider significance, and Edward Dowden's (1875) view, cited earlier (page xxxiv), that Shakespeare may have used the play to unload a weight of melancholy from himself may have been the right one. Shakespeare's depressions and perhaps disturbances were off-loaded into Jaques; and Jaques himself off-loads them finally into the 'all the world' speech, which is his last lengthy contribution. Such melancholia was probably characteristic of the Elizabethan period, its new medical knowledge of its own anatomies in fact, its speedy and heady intake of new learning, and its post-Reformation traumas. Melancholia and malcontentism were current affectations (John Marston thought Shakespeare was getting at *him*) but those of Jaques are not affected. The lovesick poet should be Orlando but, again, Shakespeare practises displacement, puts it indirectly.

The speech, though profoundly thoughtful, is also outward. It is dawning on Jaques as he goes. Jaques's earlier speeches, just considered, refer to himself (I, my, me) nearly thirty times, but this speech does so not once. The first five stages are introduced by a time-adverb followed by one-word title in every case. 'At first the infant', 'then, the whining schoolboy', 'and then the lover', 'then, a soldier', 'and then, the justice'. The last of these five is rounded off with a curious new summarising fixity: 'and so he plays his part'. Finally, for the sixth and seventh stages, this brevity of introduction is widened:

> The sixth age shifts
> Into the lean and slipper'd pantaloon,
> With spectacles on nose, and pouch on side
>
> Last scene of all,
> That ends this strange eventful history,
> Is second childishness and mere oblivion,
> Sans teeth, sans eyes, sans taste, sans everything.
>
> (ii, vii, 157–9, 163–6)

That phrase, 'this strange eventful history', sounds more like the formal conclusions to the major tragedies, when the upright calm successor who will take over the government of the destroyed state summarises what has gone before. Jaques has quietened down, and the pool can settle below the waterfall, wiser and newly instructed.

Jaques's 'blocking' thereafter, and I take Frye's term for comedy's counterforce deliberately at this point, is not unpleasant, less still an attempt to hold up any overt action in any serious way. Later in Act iii Jaques redirects his attention to Touchstone, is gently curious about the latter's impending marriage, commends him to his lord – apparently with all sincerity – and at the end simply does his round of distribution of benefits (v, iv, 185–91) and leaves. There is no 'I'll be revenged on the whole pack of you' atmosphere, as from Malvolio in *Twelfth Night*. In fact Jaques runs parallel to the play somewhat, commenting on who and what he sees, intervening as far as his over-active mind needs it. But it does seem useful generally to reintroduce the 'jakes' pun and see Jaques as taking to himself the extraneous matter the play needs to unload if the light-of-touch loves are to proceed. The temptation to see Jaques's frequently mentioned 'matter' ('foul sores of th' infected world' and the like) as the melancholic's lumber of constipated material, which has to be 'evacuated' (Burton's frequent term; see below) is hard to resist.

Of course, Jaques may loom large partly because of Shakespeare's propensity to let a character grow out of proportion to the original plan. Thus Shylock outgrew Antonio, Beatrice and Benedick outgrew Claudio and Hero, and Jaques outgrows Orlando. This last seems especially likely if, as many feel,

Jaques and Jaques de Boys were originally one character, the middle one of the three sons of Sir Rowland. That would mean that, rather than simply inventing Jaques as he invented Touchstone, Shakespeare's idea of this brother as family intellectual ran away with him. The question is of the nature of this enlargement, and why Shakespeare became so interested.

Jaques's mind – not only his mind – like that of Robert Burton in *The Anatomy of Melancholy*, that famous work of two decades later, is overweighted. It has 'a thousand similes'. Burton writes that 'I write of melancholy, by being busy to avoid melancholy. There is no greater cause of melancholy than idleness' – something Montaigne found in retirement – 'no better cure than business'; and what needs curing is 'a kind of impostume in my head which I was very desirous to be unladen of and could imagine no fitter evacuation than this' (1932, pp. 20, 21). The 'evacuation' is a teeming outpouring of unparagraphed matter almost impossible to capture without very lengthy quotation, far longer than what can be given here. The grabbing of material to produce an over-saturated mind Burton attacks in others and himself:

> They lard their lean books with the fat of others' works. *Ineruditi fures*, etc. A fault that every writer finds, as I do now, and yet faulty themselves, *trium literarum homines*, all thieves; they pilfer out of old writers to stuff up their new comments, scrape Ennius' dung-hills, and out of Democritus' pit, as I have done. By which means it comes to pass 'that not only libraries and shops are full of our putrid papers but every close-stool and jakes', *Scribunt carmina quae legunt cacantes* they serve to put under pies, to lap spice in, and to keep roast from burning. (p. 23)

The songs

Jaques's very first words in the play respond to Amiens's first song. 'More, more, I prithee more.' Virtually his last sound like a rejection: 'I am for other than for dancing measures'. He maintains a love–hate relationship with them throughout, and the dialogue with Amiens continues:

Amiens It will make you melancholy, Monsieur Jaques.
Jaques I thank it . . . I can suck melancholy out of a song,
          as a weasel sucks eggs. More, I prithee more.
Amiens My voice is ragged, I know I cannot please you.
Jaques I do not desire you to please me, I do desire you to
          sing.

                                              (II, v, 10–16)

The song–melancholy association itself is cognate with a
long tradition that goes through the fourth opening poem of
Burton's book (that poem, 'The Author's Abstraction of
Melancholy', could almost be by Jaques, the parallels are so
close), through *L'Allegro* and *Il Penseroso* on down to
Wordsworth, Tennyson, Keats and Edward Thomas. Love
and melancholy are sweet and sorrowful at once. That link is
itself found in other Shakespearian songs; for example, the
Cuckoo Song from *Love's Labour's Lost*, often pirated for our
play as we have seen. Desdemona's willow song in *Othello* (the
play's only song bar Iago's brief attempt to get Cassio drunk)
wells up from the moment of her deepest wretchedness. And in
Twelfth Night Feste makes the distinction explicit: 'Would
you have a love-song, or a song of good life?'
    More widely, of course, Shakespeare's major comedies re-
peatedly espouse music, and music's centrality to life. 'If music
be the food of love, play on' are *Twelfth Night*'s opening
words, and *The Merchant of Venice* is loaded with it and
references to it. Levi-Strauss put it that music is the central
articulation of a culture. So if Frye's theory of comedy is
correct – that it is the fullest representation of a community's
unity, getting everyone (bar perhaps the blocking agent himself on to the stage at the end and rounding the story into a
rebirth, whereas tragedy chops it off – then we would feel no
surprise at the music–comedy connection. *As You Like It*
contains more songs than any other Shakespeare play.
    The songs themselves underline the play's themes, or
themselves partake in them. They speak of man's security in
the greenwood even in winter; man's ingratitude as worse than
such cold; the return of spring; cuckoldry in apparent victory;
the celebration of wedlock. But they are also integral to the
play's nature. It is not a matter of the author planting a tune

here and there for greater entertainment. C.L. Barber (1959) pointed out how several of them descend from the holiday tradition of ritual festivity: drinking songs, love songs, songs of jollity to stave off the winter's cold. Their written texture is also of the play's texture. 'Under the greenwood tree' – that line – has as much of the alliterative density, and of the same kind, as the poetry elsewhere.

The relation of songs to whole play is very exact. First, each song has near counterparts in the text. 'Under the greenwood tree' repeats the spirit and content of Duke Senior's speech at the start of Act II. 'Blow, blow thou winter wind' continues that theme and that poetic mode; and 'Thy tooth is not so keen . . . Although thy breath be rude' just could be Amiens's own answer to Jaques's parody at II, v, 47–54. But this song also looks ahead, and that can't be Amiens. It would have to be Shakespeare himself, or, so to speak, the play's moving spirit. The line 'most friendship is feigning, most loving mere folly' seems to half-affirm/half-deny Touchstone's remark about poetry itself, that 'the truest poetry is the most feigning, and lovers are given to poetry, and what they swear in poetry may be said as lovers they do feign' (III, iii, 16–18). It links song and poetry furthermore to Touchstone's detached comments about folly itself. The songs are switch-points through which otherwise separated parts of the play signal to each other. Textual critics can pick them up, but so can good producers.

Yet most intriguing of all are the passages in the play, outside the songs, that could serve as songs. They have their own chanting movement or more extended rhythmic pulse and charm. Seng (1967), in a study of Shakespeare's songs, called *As You Like It* 'virtually a musical comedy' and some stage productions have attempted this. Wouldn't some of Rosalind's one-liners make luscious song-titles? 'Say a day, without the ever.' 'And I am your Rosalind.' 'Men have died . . . but not for love.' Orlando's words sound like the antiphons of the psalms to appear in the King James Version hardly more than a decade later: 'I shall do my friends no wrong, for I have none to lament me; the world no injury, for in it I have nothing' (I, ii, 178–80). Some of Silvius's first words sound like the pastoral love-lament they are clearly supposed to imitate (II, iv, 30–9). And in a touching moment, the Phebe who had hitherto despised him turns to him for support in her moment of being un-requited: 'Good shepherd, tell this youth what 'tis to love'. Silvius answers, and the others fill in:

Silvius	It is to be all made of sighs and tears,
	And so am I for Phebe.
Phebe	And I for Ganymede.
Orlando	And I for Rosalind.
Rosalind	And I for no woman.
Silvius	It is to be all made of faith and service,
	And so am I for Phebe.
Phebe	And I for Ganymede.
Orlando	And I for Rosalind.
Rosalind	And I for no woman.
Silvius	It is to be all made of fantasy,
	All made of passion and all made of wishes,
	All adoration, duty and observance
	All humbleness, all patience and impatience,
	All purity, all trial, all observance;
	And so am I for Phebe.
Phebe	And so am I for Ganymede.
Orlando	And so am I for Rosalind.
Rosalind	And so am I for no woman.

(v, ii, 83–101)

Rosalind's subsequent round of promises is the same; so are the verses of Hymen; so, differently, is the set piece of Corin's defence of the country back at iii, ii, 71–5; and indeed Jaques's seven ages speech is a kind of extended cantata in its formal divisions and sombre regular phrasing. For that last reason I would see Jaques's own round of distributed benefits at the end, as his conversion into the song he all along wanted, even while he believes himself to be rejecting such dancing measures for ever:

(to Duke S.)	You to your former honour I bequeath,
	Your patience and your virtue well deserve it.
(to Orl.)	You to a love that your true faith doth merit.
(to Oli.)	You to your land and love and great allies:
(to Sil.)	You to a long and well-deserved bed:

(To Touch.)   And you to wrangling, for thy loving voyage
  Is but for two months victuall'd. So to your pleasures.
  I am for other than for dancing measures.

(v, iv, 185–92)

And, of course, there are Orlando's verses too.

Orlando

Orlando is perhaps the play's main illustration of a point made all along about the balance between language and character. He can appeal, in some ways; in others he is hardly 'he' at all. He isn't all there.

The post-war critics couldn't agree about Orlando. There were the standard starting-points, of course: romantic hero; Petrarchan lover; physically beautiful young man. Over-the-top admirers of Rosalind saw Orlando as a dupe. Bertrand Evans saw Orlando as the most admirable of Shakespeare's comic heroes, listing as rivals Proteus, Bassanio, Claudio and Bertram. Yet, according to Evans, Orlando also remains oblivious. Thanks to her 'unrivalled native gifts' (*sic*) Rosalind has all understanding, Orlando none. Yet Evans felt some sympathy for him: 'Rarely flattering to his comic heroes, Shakespeare treats Orlando abominably!' (1960, pp. 92, 95). But if Orlando is 'admirable' too, the picture may be more complex than Evans allowed.

There was equal uncertainty where Orlando stood as lovesick lover. For McFarland (1972) the lovesickness is literally sick, coming over as 'moist and ludicrous', and Silvius is a deliberate parody. For Harold Jenkins (1967) by contrast Silvius is needed precisely to deflect superfluous ridicule from Orlando, otherwise Rosalind's love for Orlando would not be convincing enough beyond the level of farce. And surely too the play could hardly have stood the intensities of three ego-expressives at once; Orlando, Silvius and Jaques together. Leggatt (1974) came somewhere between these two positions, suggesting that Orlando writes like a Petrarchan lover but doesn't seem, all round, to be one. In short, Leggatt saw a flaw, if not too serious a one, in Shakespeare's construction and characterisation.

Feminist criticism has broadened our view on the matter. Instead of now simply eulogising Rosalind from a safe distance, a closer analysis has developed of the role of the Shakespearian heroine in the mature comedies, with the result that the required hero can be seen in relation to that. Linda Bamber has suggested that the heroes of these comedies (Orsino, Orlando, even Benedick) 'seem a little dazed and inept, as though they had wandered in from some other play' (1982, p. 41). That seems perceptive. The usual feminist emphasis is that these plays are Shakespeare's attempt to give woman expression by – usually – putting her in disguise so that she can say and be what otherwise only the hero could say and be. (The more radical feminist view is that male Shakespeare could only go so far with this.) If that view is correct, then the hero has to be at a break-even point between too cardboard a figure (not worth her attention at all) and too full-bodied a figure (wrapping her into a local relationship which would block the desired generalities). Does Orlando fit this?

Orlando has no *project* to find and win Rosalind. He hasn't ever Bassanio's real, if mixed, ambition based on exploitation-cum-attraction. He has no soliloquy saying 'I'll-do-this-I'll-do-that'. When he has met her after the wrestling, he merely says 'but heavenly Rosalind!' and the scene is over. And until he meets Rosalind again – and it is the equivalent of almost two acts later – every action and word we get from him is to do with the support and saving of his old servant Adam, who, like Lear's fool, departs the play midway through. Even so, this time that departure happens precisely because Orlando has got him to Arden, got him food, and – presumably – integrated him into the group of Duke Senior's foresters. The last time we see Adam he is safely under the Duke's kind wing:

> Good old man,
> Thou art right welcome as thy master is.
> Support him by the arm. Give me your hand
> And let me all your fortunes understand.
>   (II, vii, 200–3)

We never hear of Adam again.

Orlando's verses, pinned to the trees, are neither introduced by him nor greatly followed up. All that happens at III, ii, 1–10, is that Orlando pins up his verse, recites it and leaves. He never says why he writes them, what he thinks of them, how he pines or anything else. When Rosalind later asks him about them he is abrupt and equivocal (III, ii, 387). He claims to be 'love-shaked', but it is one word, and his more suicidal expressions early on (I, ii, 176–82; II, iii, 63) seemed more spontaneous. When he next appears in his own right, so to put it, he is wittily resisting Jaques's tilts in a brief encounter. Rosalind and Celia overhear this and accost him. The wooing scenes are under way.

Orlando has his wrestling, of course. Indeed he has not one fight but four, at least if you include the charge at the feast party of outlaws, where his heroics in taking on them all are made superfluous by the Duke's upstaging gentility. But Shakespeare plays down the wrestling. He may even have had a remark of Castiglione's in mind:

> if anyone is anxious to wrestle with peasants, then he ought, in my opinion, to do it casually, out of *noblesse oblige* . . . and he *should be almost certain of winning*, or else not take part at all, for it is too sad and shocking, and quite un-dignified, when a gentleman is seen to be beaten by a peasant, especially in a wrestling match. (Castiglione, 1967, p. 117, my emphasis)

Orlando's real significance I believe lies elsewhere.

It is his response to the Duke that is the revealing key. 'Speak you so gently?' Orlando's inscribed concern with speech recurs frequently. His response to Rosalind's final enforced 'magical' promises is 'speak'st thou in sober meanings?' His responses to Adam are similarly explicitly to what has been said: 'Why, what's the matter?' 'Why how now Adam? No greater heart in thee?' It is Orlando who opens the play with a vigorous, alliterative speech, his longest, and is allotted two verbal encounters, with Oliver and with Jaques as just noted (I, i, 29–51 and III, ii, 249–89). In both of these a point-by-point verbal contest is engaged, with little yielded as approachable and vulnerable. The more interesting it is then that his falling for Rosalind is conceived of as his own failure to articulate.

'Can I not say, "I thank you"? . . . What passion hangs these weights upon my tongue? I cannot speak to her, yet she urg'd conference' (I, ii, 239, 247–8). And indeed this talk of Orlando's, though hardly hollow or sham, is not seen by others as fully robust. Celia, no doubt with her own motivation, says there is no truth in him. It is a different perspective; we cannot credit Celia while at the same time suspecting her too of some blockage. Yet the feeling about Orlando persists. He must enable Rosalind, in this most articulate and conversational of plays, to be the expansive one when they fully encounter. And when she reveals who she is at the play's end, he is silenced.

This silencing of a main character in Shakespeare is often a key to how far something of importance for that character is irreversibly over, for better or worse. At the news that his ships have come home, Antonio (*Merchant of Venice*) says 'I am dumb'. Finally detected and arrested, Iago says, 'From this time forth I never will speak word'. For Hamlet 'The rest is silence', his speech at the very moment of death meaning that even when the poison's effects were irreversible the words of the prince were poignant for continued dramatic event and political significance in the ears of his followers. With Orlando it is the closure on his articulation itself that counts. He has to think what he has said.

This is hardly the whole story about Orlando, for his other actions, too, build up the necessary picture of his maleness as that which an unservile woman might still approach. It is real and symbolic at once. He fights, really but also symbolically: in a Cain–Abel context; for an old man's food; against a much heavier professional wrestler; and, most of all, as Nancy Hayles (1979) has pointed out, against the symbolically saturated creatures of lioness and serpent. This last is real in that he does save Oliver, but symbolic in that those animals seem to carry psychoanalytical overtones and imply defeat, as Hayles suggests, of both castration fear and female engulfment. Yet whether he convinces us that he is a potential partner for Rosalind – at least as far as that is needed in the wooing story we have – lies in how far he is challenging and worth respecting at once, along a dimension she can identify with. He may have 'chestnut hair' and the rest, but he has also to be adjacent to articulation itself, so that she can win in it, love it and take over from it. She can do this partly because he is 'like a dropped acorn', fallen from the trees that are talking's source, while vulnerable and infantile beside them; partly because he doesn't know who she is, who Ganymede is. In being silenced he finds that out.

· 3 ·

Disguise

At this point the discussion becomes more convoluted. When Rosalind disguises she compounds the fact that all acting is performance anyway, with the further complication that in our day Rosalind is normally played by a woman, whereas Shakespeare had to assume an adolescent male took the part, as indeed was the case for all his female parts. Furthermore, while women characters have already worn male disguise in *Twelfth Night*, *Two Gentlemen of Verona* and *The Merchant of Venice*, *As You Like It* is unique in that Rosalind also plays another part, the male youth Ganymede, who then plays or re-plays her own self, folding the matter back in upon itself while giving it an extra twist. Finally the diverse conceptions of disguise, cross-dressing, androgyny and transvestitism break up the straightforward matter of gender concealment into a sub-group of yet further possibilities.

We disguise much of the time anyway, to look tough, rich, respectable, Westernised, poor or pathetic. There is also a continuum between the aim to conceal what we are and the aim to reveal it. Men in the 1960s didn't grow long hair in order to be mistaken for girls, but to suggest unisex identification, or emancipation more generally. It is curious today that while women have commonly adopted what was male clothing – trousers, caps, rugby shirts – you don't see men in skirts and stockings or lace blouses without assuming they are fully transvestite. Disguise would seem to be something more specific.

In Elizabethan England females disguised themselves as males, or were presented as doing so on stage, from a number of motives: a) to cover their female parts and avoid lascivious approach; b) to get male privileges; c) to express defiance at patriarchy; and d) to get an erotic kick. Rosalind and Celia – and Julia in *Two Gentlemen of Verona* – disguise for the first reason given here (*TGV* II, vii, 39–43; *AYLI* I, iii, 106–10). A number of feminist critics (Howard, 1988, *et al.*) also ascribe the second motive to Rosalind and Celia, in the sense that those two thereby become liberated to speak freely, as men may already. The third motive, not unconnected, was that of the gangs of male-dressed women who roamed London in the late sixteenth century, and were attacked by offended males for their turpitude, as in the now well-known pamphlet of 1620, *Hic Mulier* (anon., published 1973). The fourth motive was the gist of the Puritan attacks on the theatre itself, as result of which boys were used for acting instead of women, not that this prevented titillations of a more homosexual nature arising instead. But, even if we see (as suggested earlier) some degree of phallic envy in Rosalind, and some lesbianism in Celia, it is hardly more than latent. So the first two of these four motives for cross-dressings look the likely ones for Rosalind. But they are also the two in which full disguise, as concealment, is essential. The fourth does not need concealment, although it is normally likely, and the third positively demands display as a protest against female suppression.

So, if Rosalind is disguising her womanhood from Orlando – the very person in the long run she most wants to know it – what credence can we give to the androgyny theories that have been widely elaborated in recent years as deep in the sub-structure of Shakespeare's mature, full-heroine comedies? Are Rosalind and those like her at last enjoying being fully women, normally under wraps through the subordinate role they normally get? Or are they for once enjoying being men, by inwardly at least savouring associating with men on basis of

gender-equality? It is often said now that Rosalind can be
fully woman at last because this is re-routed round through
Ganymede. But even if this is true, a level of subtlety in the play
is surely lost if we aren't awakened to the inner mixture of
gender role and experience Rosalind must be thought of as
gaining by playing both female and male at once. The further
question is raised, then, of how far gender is itself socially
constructed, as the modern pro-androgyny faction normally
suggests. If Rosalind's physical sex does not change, is her
response merely political, merely a sense of rights? Is she not
experiencing a bit of malehood in her doublet and hose, or at
least some kind of gender neutrality for social equality to hold
her allegiance as well? The extreme sorority of the feminist
movement might argue an equal-but-different (or superior-
but-different) position anyway, but they would hardly go
along with Rosalind's yearning for Orlando in the first place.
Added to this is the question of Shakespeare's own approach;
whether he was supporting female emancipation or silently
subverting it (by bringing the women back to marriage at each
play's end).

The renewed attention to the boy actor in recent years makes
for further difficulties. It is underlined that there are four
layers: the boy-actor, Rosalind, Ganymede and 'Rosalind' to
Orlando. In fact, there are only three layers of performance:
the boy playing Rosalind, Rosalind playing Ganymede and
Ganymede playing 'Rosalind'. More importantly, these act-
ings appear on scrutiny to have quite different degrees in
them of the 'disguise' element we have already considered.

There is a boy-actor. Let us call him Basil (Boy Actor
Simulation In Love). Basil plays Rosalind, but everyone knows
it is a boy, and indeed an actor; the 'disguise' is not a concealment. Rosalind, however, plays Ganymede, but within
the different world of the play; and this is part concealment,
part not. Within the play's world Celia and Touchstone know
who she is, and who her 'sister Aliena' is. No one else does.
Below that line, however, the layers of acting divide. For
Ganymede now plays Orlando's original lady-love, whom we
might call Moira (Male Orlando's Idealised 'Rosalind' Acted).
So we have the four: Basil playing Rosalind playing Ganymede
playing Moira. But Ganymede is still visible to Orlando as

Ganymede as well, and still within the same level of reality, the play's world. A final component to the situation is added by Orlando's position at this stage. If Ganymede is acting Moira to Orlando's full knowledge (just as Basil is acting Rosalind to the audience's full knowledge) then Orlando is acting too; he is at least playing along, with his 'then love me Rosalind' and (to Celia) 'pray thee marry us' (IV, i, 109, 120).

At a political level furthermore, if the very presence of the boy-actor reminded the women in Shakespeare's Elizabethan audience of their own suppression more generally, then that dimension has now departed, to some degree at least, when we see the Vanessa Redgraves and Fiona Shaws play the role today. (From one point of view, no doubt frivolous, this seems sad. As Juliet Dusinberre says (1975, p. 253), boys make bewitching girls, girls make lumbering youths.) So we have to choose between these two periods for interpretation of political significance, or turn to a different approach. I don't myself doubt the interest and truth of the political dimension, though I do wonder what Shakespeare made from it. But it is not the only dimension on which these cross-dressing plays can be read. There is, for example, the Foucault dimension of the raising of sexuality into existence by the very act of the articulation of its suppression (see Foucault, 1979). This historical process seems to parallel the way our play brings the woman's body into prominence by the act of hiding it, by disguise, from male approaches. But it seems to me that the approach most likely to gather all these strands of disguise and its ramification into a manageable idea is the one which makes the theatre, and acting, central themselves. It takes Jaques literally.

All these aspects of disguise – cross-dressing, boy-actors, comic doublings (Rosalind as Ganymede's twin), concealment, role-playing and the rest – are performances, all part of the theatrical world. The idea that all the world's a stage is explicitly highlighted by disguise, role-playing and even dressing. Normally disguise itself is as inherently suspenseful a situation for the audience as is, for example, whether a burglar will be caught or a lover interrupted. The small tension between what the person is and what they pretend to be, keeps the watching mind in gear, at the ready, waiting for developments from a possible disclosure, even when nothing is happening. But with Rosalind it is different. When the disguised person merely plays her original self, that tension is suspended. It is kept; it doesn't dissolve, because the actor does re-route herself round through another part, unknown to the observer on stage. But the action is stopped by the blocking circle of actor imitating herself. There is a void at the heart of the action, awaiting movement which doesn't come until she is ready for it. After all, Rosalind could have acted another woman and then played her own bed-trick. But she didn't. And because she is not acting another, no other is implicated. This takes the event into the heart and very principle of acting. It is sheer acting, sheer role-playing; playing oneself. The response from others present is, as the audience knows, not what matters. Orlando can only take so much of this pretence, and Celia just waits for Rosalind to finish. It is Rosalind who stands or falls, arrests or grows.

What does Rosalind do in this arrested space of her own making? We can come to that, but I'll throw my cap and towel into the ring at this point. I think that Shakespeare loved Rosalind, as Dante is said to have loved Beatrice and as, in some way perhaps, Dickens loved Little Dorrit. Rosalind was at least the fourth woman he had dressed as a man in his work, and, as Virginia Woolf said, his was the prototype of the androgynous mind. His males are inadequate, his women dominant whether generous or wicked. Rosalind seemed, in Lodge, a chance for him to write her in with the action stopped so that he could look at her in a full way, the camera frames seized. He wanted to enter her with his whole self; but he could not be so ungallant as to proclaim such conquest, so he put a double disguise over her as defence against his own intrusions. As Jan Kott (1967) said, Orlando doesn't know Rosalind is there, but she *is* there. Whether there is a real heterosexual meeting between Orlando and Rosalind is an open question. After *Romeo and Juliet* Shakespeare did not write another full love-story. The political implications of either cross-dressing or subordination didn't concern Shakespeare except as material; what he revealed about his own ideologies is another matter.

Rosalind's body

She has none; but the wounded deer has. So have Orlando and the lioness who wounds him. Is Shakespeare remotely suggesting the body is to be ignored? Or that in a truly civilised and green world all wounding and all blood will have gone; no tooth and claw? Shakespeare loved minds, perhaps, or so expresses it.

Was Rosalind a virgin? The one place where we might find the answer is at v, ii, 116 when Rosalind makes her round of promises to Orlando, Silvius and Phebe. To Orlando she says 'I will satisfy you, if ever I satisfied man, and you shall be married tomorrow'. The past tense might imply, as one would say, former relationships. And broadly Rosalind's tone of confidence and competence in the wooing scenes might strongly suggest necessary experiences. Yet the imaginative realm of the play won't let us particularise as to what such a man would have been like, or – more significant – even allow the existence of any such particularisation. In real life, given such a situation, one might wonder what the bloke was like. But Rosalind exists in a closed play; you can't 'wonder what the bloke was like' for to do so would be to invent another character within the play's fabric, which is impossible. An enclosed, finished fictional world of the play can't entertain an extra person, inserted from another world. To that extent the ethereal quality of the play, much beloved of the Victorians, does seem to insist itself.

The only conceivable candidate, therefore, was and is William Shakespeare. If he thought of her as not a virgin, then she wasn't one, and he was responsible. Since he doesn't say, the question, so far as it presses, hangs forever in balance, and again surely we are free to delight, perhaps required to delight, that it can only have been the one person who had gone with her to Arden and known her there, playing many parts in such times.

Do we know what she looked like? He knew her, but hardly tells us. Even where he briefly does, it is contradictory. At i, iii, 111 she is 'more than common tall', but at i, ii, 262 we were told by Le Beau that 'the taller is his daughter', that is Duke Frederick's daughter Celia. Unless Celia was a giantess this is either a mistake in transcription (the view of most editors) or, as I perversely suggest, Shakespeare planting false clues, something he just may have done on the virginity question. This one really *is* as we like it, a phrase the play's commentators must normally labour to avoid, so temptingly does it repeatedly offer itself. We don't ask, as of the number of Lady Macbeth's children, whether Rosalind was a virgin, for it is open but not blank; tenuously half-way; and we don't want to know what she looked like.

This last is a matter of the language, which leads us always sinuously around avoiding any matter of lily-white breasts, lovely blue eyes, slender legs or anything else of the kind one sees in much of Spenser and in Marlowe's *Hero and Leander*. In both of those poets the verbal allure is less voiced than physically present, sumptuously erotic:

> Her goodly eyes lyke Saphyres shining bright,
> Her forehead yvory white,
> Her cheeks lyke apples which the sun hath rudded,
> Her lips lyke cherryes charming men to byte,
> Her brest lyke to a bowle of creame uncrudded,
> Her paps lyke lyllies budded,
> Her snowie necke lyke to a marble towre,
> And all her bodie lyke to a pallace fayre
> (Spenser, *Epithalamion* 171–8)

– which on Rosalind would have been absurd whether 'heavenly' or not. Such standing-back regard by the poet is nowhere found in Shakespeare's play. Rather, Shakespeare gives Rosalind a general sexuality in various ways. There is the occasional bodily reference which comes through jocular dialogue to which Rosalind never directly responds:

Rosalind   . . . I prithee take the cork out of thy mouth, that I may drink thy tidings.
Celia   So you may put a man in your belly.
Rosalind   Is he of God's making? What manner of man? Is his head worth a hat? Or his chin worth a beard?
(III, ii, 199–203)

This is a good case of the extraordinary technique of indirection the play evinces (another is that Audrey of all people
asks the big questions about poetry), for Rosalind's body is the
one in question, in this scene most of all. But this passage is also
the one where Rosalind is put before us with her own desire
heightened, and a musk of sexual excitement gathers:

Celia	And a chain, that you once wore, about his neck. Change you colour?
Rosalind	I prithee who?
Celia	O Lord, Lord! It is a hard matter for friends to meet; but mountains may be remov'd with earth-quakes, and so encounter.
Rosalind	Nay, but who is it?
Celia	Is it possible?
Rosalind	Nay, I prithee now, with most petitionary vehemence, tell me who it is.
Celia	O wonderful, wonderful . . . !

And Rosalind pesters Celia for more and more information,
but with almost panting volubility herself: 'One inch of delay
more is a South Sea of discovery. I prithee tell me who it is
quickly, and speak apace. I would thou couldst stammer, that
thou mightst pour this concealed man out of thy mouth, as
wine comes out of a narrow-mouthed bottle . . .'

According to Barbara Everett (1990), Shakespeare's characters are forms not persons, but, however, being perceived
by the author as, and somehow bodily, embodied. But the
embodiment of Rosalind comes out of her own mouth, without the distance of Cleopatra's lustrous barge (an indirection
for herself) or Pandarus's news of Cressida's state when she is
just coming to meet Troilus:

> She does so blush, and fetches her wind so short, as if she were
> frayed with a spirit! I'll fetch her: It is the prettiest villain;
> she fetches her breath as short as a new-ta'en sparrow.
>
> (*Troilus and Cressida* iii, ii, 29–33)

If the play is indeed riddled with puns and *doubles entendres*,
both sexual and otherwise, it makes for a seamless verbal web

by which sexuality, and perhaps androgyny, pervade without exact placing of unique bodily detail on to separate characters. It makes the play, and Rosalind herself, porous, X-rayed; we needn't stray about on the skin to know her that way. I think incidentally that this may account for the credibility we can easily allow in believing that Orlando never recognises Rosalind. It wasn't that Elizabethans, lacking the high-tech photographic experience we have now, didn't know who they were talking to. They were attentive enough to facial detail, as the friar in *Much Ado About Nothing* makes clear:

> Hear me a little;
> For I have only been silent so long,
> And given way unto this course of fortune,
> By noting of the lady. I have mark'd
> A thousand blushing apparitions
> To start into her face, a thousand innocent shames
> In angel whiteness beat away those blushes,
> And in her eye there hath appear'd a fire,
> To burn the errors that these princes hold
> Against her maiden truth. Call me a fool;
> Trust not my reading nor my observations,
> Which with experimental seal doth warrant
> The tenor of my book; trust not my age,
> My reverence, calling, nor divinity,
> If this sweet lady lie not guiltless here
> Under some biting error.
> *(Much Ado About Nothing* iv, i, 155–69)

Elizabethan preoccupation with eye-darts, blushes and the rest seems unlikely to have gone along with literal misrecognition of the actual face of the individual so emoting. Rather the switch of role symbolically put on by disguise was accepted, or certainly is in this play where all is a stage, as more significant than the incidental bodily differences individuals might have inherited. In *As You Like It* it is words themselves that are androgynous, or gendered. The double meanings pass quickly over in bush, nest, hind, heart, cote, bestow, cattle, misuse, forest, doublet, ripe, sister, wine, part, prick, Ganymede and many others. They saturate our awareness of the human physical presence in general and, of the characters in some cases, their alerted feelings. They undermine myth, whose double meanings are not verbal but palpable, animal, symbolic.

Rosalind's wooing

Rosalind neither woos Orlando nor acts the part of Moira. Rosalind draws Orlando inward to a sexual play-acting he always treats as such (he returns an hour late and then politely leaves) but which for all we know is not even heterosexual; and she never pretends to be Moira at all. Rather she tells Orlando what he needs to do to win Moira. As Rubinstein points out (1984, p. 123), 'heavenly' has the implication of homosexual, in that Plato contrasted heavenly love with earthly as that between man–man and man–woman. One reading of Orlando's silence at the play's end is disappointment. He has found this youth Ganymede rather attractive, and Ganymede is gone. His romanticising with his verses was merely the correct 'young man' thing to do; his heart was hardly in it.

The wooing has two phases. In the first (III, ii, 292–423) Rosalind persuades Orlando to agree to let this 'Ganymede' before him teach him how to woo and win his desired lady. In the second phase (IV, i, 36–190) she actually does this, although there turns out to have been more and less to it. *The first phase is based on titillation, the second on language.* The technique throughout the first phase is to intrigue Orlando by indirection. She repeatedly says the opposite of the truth, knowing Orlando knows the truth, so that even to raise the opposite is to raise a contrast and so hold his attention, his tension. He is drawn in to the orbit of the language, of its affirmations, so that his mind and feelings can't escape them. Even when what she says is not strictly untrue, it is underlyingly sexual, yet in such a way as not to raise suspicion of direct approach. His enticement is purely erotic.

As soon as she has asked him the time and he has replied that there is no clock in the forest, her answer is an untruth, the truth of which she herself knows is known to Orlando. 'Then there is no true lover in the forest.' He is that lover, as she knows. She then offers to tell him about time, not just

generally, but its four speeds, a rich fabric of potential information about human foibles. The next erotilla is her answer when,
now thoroughly intrigued, Orlando asks where she lives.
'Where dwell you pretty youth?' 'In the skirts of the forest',
she replies enticingly, 'like fringe upon a petticoat', but quickly
adds 'thank God I am not a woman', a possibility Orlando may
not have thought of but will immediately start incubating:
'. . . to be touched with so many giddy offences as he hath
generally taxed their whole sex withal'. The next move is the
extended pretence (III, ii, 349–74) that Orlando is *not* the lover
pinning verses to trees, and the disdainful suggestion that he is
hardly dressed for the part (368–71). She has thus raised the
whole wooing subject while never seeming to do so herself, a
technique used to far more sinister effect by Iago throughout
the third act of *Othello*, to a point where the Moor is knotted
up with a nightmare tangle of what he believes to be his own
thoughts.

Rosalind ends on the sexually potent 'come' (415, 422 – it
recurs at IV, i, 65), the refrain more plangent from Juliet when
her lover was not listening:

> Come night, come Romeo, come thou day in night,
> For thou wilt lie upon the wings of night
> Whiter than new snow upon a raven's back.
> Come gentle night, come loving black-brow'd night,
> Give me my Romeo . . .
> (*Romeo and Juliet* III, ii, 17–21)

Orlando does 'come', but only 'within an hour of my promise',
and that speech-act failure is cue to his ensuing entanglement,
in the second 'wooing' phase (IV, i, 36–190), in every kind of
talk. Again, he has already started at a disadvantage. Not to
elaborate each, there is the broken promise (42), the 'slander' of
his wife (59), the naming of 'Rosalind' (62–3), the demand that
he woo (65) and the interchange about talking and kissing
(66–9), the talk of orators (72–3), the suit pun (82–3), the
affirmations of saying (87–8), the accusations of male lies (89–
103, especially 101), the request for favours (108) – all leading
to the culmination in the mock-marriage (117–31), itself a form
wholly of words though one now moving dangerously close to

irreversible intimacies. But Rosalind does not leave it there.
Orlando must say how long he would have his wife (135), hear
how she will clamour and laugh (143, 147); and the whole is
then summarised by Rosalind herself in a self-knowing mock-
ery of her own volubility: 'You shall never take her [your wife]
without her answer, unless you take her without her tongue'
(162–4). The conclusion is disarming in its success, as Rosalind
preposterously declares that 'That flattering tongue of yours
won me' and ends with a spate of speech-acts which lead
Orlando into essential courteous withdrawal:

> *Rosalind* By my troth, and in good earnest, and so God
> mend me, and by all pretty oaths that are not dangerous, if
> you break one jot of your promise, or come one minute
> behind your hour, I will think you the most pathetical
> break-promise, and the most hollow lover, and the most
> unworthy of her you call Rosalind, that may be chosen out
> of the gross band of the unfaithful: therefore beware my
> censure and keep your promise.
> *Orlando* With no less religion than if thou wert indeed my
> Rosalind. So adieu.
>
> (IV, i, 178–88)

Sexual enticement and the traps of language: Orlando is not
wooed but entangled. Yet the language is generous; one
couldn't really imagine the scene ending other than agreeably,
although the degrees between fall-about laughter (Celia included) and the wistfulness of Rosalind in her speeches about
male unfaithfulness (IV, i, 89–103, 138–48) may vary considerably as to how we imagine them. This might depend on what
we feel about Orlando's entanglement. Is he so fated? What
does he think this youth Ganymede is after? Or is he himself
enticed toward that relationship, his own Moira fading? The
mock-marriage is a conclusion, the game can't really go on; yet
nothing has happened. The marriage was a fantasy. From his
clinical studies Winnicott observed (1974, p. 32) that, with
fantasy unlike with imagination, when you return to reality,
nothing has happened. The titillations were indirect and the
language-games rolled around, but where are we? Nowhere
but with the happy question of uncategoric, indistinct gender:

a boy-playing-girl-playing-boy, a boy-playing-boy, and a boy-playing-girl; one talking his/her head off, one answering moderately, one silent.

According to the founder-sociologist Georg Simmel, the dyad or interaction between two is characterised by triviality and intimacy. If true, then wooing is entrapped in the character of the dyad – whether of wooers or not – and all interaction between two is a kind of wooing itself, unless formalities are observed and constructed. One couldn't ask for more comment on our sexually ambiguous natures and situations.

Rosalind the hetero

The silent one (now *there's* a girl one might pin poems to trees for) has taken a lot; a lot too much, some critics have argued, among them Ralph Berry, Bernard Evans and Dr Johnson himself. Few agree today (though many sympathise with Celia) but perhaps the question needs a look. For it is deeply germane to the gender question, or so I shall argue.

Here is the case against Rosalind:

1. She is self-pitying (I, iii, 88, III, iv, 1–4).
2. She is vain: useless and faint-hearted about going to Arden until the self-indulgence of dressing-up is suggested (I, iii, 104–27) (Leggatt, 1974, p. 194, is surely wrong).
3. She brings talk back to herself (II, iv, 57–8, III, ii, 215–16, 225–6).
4. She doesn't reveal herself to her father, despite the joy it would presumably have given him (III, iv, 31–5); in fact she seems disdainful of him (34).
5. As indeed of everyone else, apart from Orlando; she never praises, never thanks. On occasion she is downright rude.
6. She never stops nattering (*passim*).
7. She is an interfering busybody (with Silvius and Phebe: III, iv, 55; then III, v, 34–63).
8. She betrays Celia's loyalty and friendship just when it suits her, despite that Celia's accompaniment of her to exile was voluntary.

9. She is a trickster and a cheat, with Oliver (IV, iii, 172) as well as Orlando.
10. She swoons at blood, despite all the manly boasts. When she gets desperate, it is unedifying (IV, iii, 161, V, ii, 25–6).
11. Not once, even at the end (unless V, ii, 70 is such an occasion), does she tell Orlando she loves him.

This is a formidable list. But – aside from its omissions (as well as being amusing, Rosalind is caring, it would seem: II, iv, 3–7; II, iv, 41–2, 67 and 89; III, v, 58; IV, i, 106) – it also omits the vital dimension of self-knowledge and self-monitoring one may imagine in her, which would throw quite a different light across all that is said. The play as self-knowing, as about coming to learn, is validly seen on that front if no other. But it is more than that, and at a qualitatively different level. For my list would presume a 'Rosalind' with a character and biography the play doesn't warrant. This 'Rosalind' is furthermore female in traditional mode, one which, insofar as we can impute intention to Shakespeare in this way at all (and in a play of this one's title), would entail a prior assumption of gender roles which the play, on at least some perfectly legitimate readings, constantly subverts. The difficulty, paradoxically, is brought out as much by those feminist critics who would try to qualify the degree of Shakespeare's pro-feminine stance. Thus Clara Claiborne Park (in Lenz *et al.*, 1983, pp. 100–16), acknowledging the power and autonomy in Shakespeare's main heroines, says that even so his – and perhaps other – young men are vulnerable to too much feminine assertiveness, so that a way had to be found to mitigate this. Portia therefore gives herself into wifely submission to Bassanio before she tricks him over the court scene and the rings; and Beatrice must 'stand condemn'd', as she herself says, before her pride and scorn may continue. Rosalind has more autonomy than any other heroine – it is uniquely *her* play – in the Elizabethan canon (Park does not mention *The Duchess of Malfi*). But, as Park's editors say as well (p. 5), even Rosalind's effect has to be muted. For Marilyn French (1983, p. 113) Rosalind must not offend her audience. These critics point to the wedding at the end. The games are over and Rosalind will submit to her lord.

Both these views, the suspiciously male-sounding anti-Rosalind view of the immediate post-war period and the feminist defence that Elizabethan mores couldn't allow such insubordination in 'shrews' or anyone else, postulate a traditional gender-role differentiation, with its domination and submission. So indeed does the earlier fond, male view (e.g. Dover Wilson) of Rosalind as 'capable', having everything in her control, and so on. What the 'marriages' at the end entail is a matter to which I want to return, but for the present I suggest that Rosalind is a little like Phebe, but with this difference, that 'Rosalind' – the Rosalind figure – transcends Phebe completely, to a point where she overflows the gender distinction altogether, within which Phebe is so firmly trapped.

Rosalind the spellbinder

As Dusinberre (1975) and Barber (1959) have underlined, the woman in disguise is a reveller in her own masque; mistress of misrule until marriage and rain (there is none in Arden) stop it.

Rosalind is banished; she is already a marked character. Duke Frederick ominously tells Celia: 'She is too subtle for thee, and her smoothness,/ Her very silence, and her patience/ Speak to the people and they pity her' (I, iii, 73–5). Rosalind has already placed a talisman, a gold chain, round Orlando's neck, binding him to her. In Arden she walks up to the men one by one, Corin, Orlando, Jaques; and when in between she approaches Phebe, that girl is mesmerised into love. Disguised, Rosalind draws Orlando into the intricacies of her inferential talk about love, and takes him into a marriage ceremony with curious implications, and possible legality (Lathem, 1975, Appendix B). When her swooning threatens to bring back the real world she tells Orlando of the 'magician, most profound in his art' (v, ii, 61) whom she knew in childhood and by whose skill she will make all things even in love. In a gentle, subdued chant she tells all this to the pairs of lovers; in another, the next day, she completes the spell's implications and demonstrates their culmination (v, ii, 111–22; v, iv, 115–16, 121–3). In the play's epilogue, she 'conjures' the women in the audience toward liking the play and to love in general.

In *A Midsummer Night's Dream* there was no disguised woman weaving spells; rather, the women were themselves under spells, and returned from the moonlight to growth of awareness when released from that state. The failure to see was not because of the object (disguised woman) but in the subject (the woman under the spell). The nature description in *A Midsummer Night's Dream* thus could be exact and colourful, for it goes direct to the audience: Ralegh was right. But Rosalind is no witch or woodland sprite. There is not a phrase in the play to suggest that option. On the contrary, *pretending* to magic is just one more of Rosalind's strategies. Furthermore she is doing nothing wrong, for she merely leads Orlando toward the very thing he incessantly says he wants – leading him forward yet preventing undue precipitousness too. Rather, her controlling actions reconcile good and evil, comic pairings, the sexes, the brothers, the country and the court. Beckman (1978) has discussed this *concordia discors* and sees it as essentially borne out through marriage. Traditional critics saw a Christian motif in the play too, and certainly there are traces; for instance, Silvius's rhapsody on love is a romanticised version of 1 Corinthians 13. But is it marriage that effects this reconcilement?

One may as easily see androgyny as reconciling the sexes. Howard (1988) suggests that an androgyny privileging males (women seen as merely lesser men) was at work in Elizabethan England, and that the challenge to this by women's defiant cross-dressing led to the authoritarian need for gender construction, the ideology by which it could be shown that women had subordinate roles justified by difference. As Dusinberre argues (1975, especially pp. 1–19), the humanistic strain of Erasmus and More, attesting to the equal capability of the woman's mind for educational expansion, led equally to this reaction. Today the androgynous argument is used to support the view that gender is normally socially constructed – in favour, of course, of males. True enough as far as it goes, but it makes androgyny into a support-argument in a political cause, whereas if any truth of human gender does lie in androgyny, then that is surely what is important, that is where the focus of our attention might be expected to go.

It is probably therefore more fruitful to see how the sexual and gender signs woven into Rosalind are presented, along with the several degrees to which they tie to herself personally and to people generally. It would be excessive to say *Rosalind* is androgynous; that argument would mean that she was hermaphrodite, epicene, bisexual. The race is androgynous, or otherwise, as the case may be. Many critics make a prior assumption of sex–gender as clear separation, leading to a subordination demanded of women. They then divide, insisting either that this is plain unjust (equal but different) or unjust because illogical (equal and same, equal because androgynous). Linda Bamber's stimulating and sympathetic book (1982) accords to Shakespeare not full feminism, but acknowledgement of women as 'Other' in a dialectic with feminism which is 'persistent, various, surprising and wholehearted' (p. 5). That is generous indeed, but what if Shakespeare did not see women as so 'other'?

The further complication of the boy-actors, already mentioned, is severally interpreted by several critics (e.g. Jardine, 1983; Greenblatt, 1988), again informatively but somewhat according to varying political disposition. Roughly speaking, if one sees the matter politically, then the playwrights used Basil to show that women are as good as men while still women. If one was more sexual in disposition, then the intertwining of the boy-actor with the woman-role (compounded in *As You Like It*, of course) attracts attention as to the degree of androgyny and bisexuality implied. The actress Juliet Stevenson – not alone in this – states that when Rosalind is dressed as Ganymede she can be 'most truly herself'. But that is ambiguous, it begs the question. Does it mean that, trapped in a women-subordinated world, she can only be truly woman when disguised as man, and only then can her non-male, fully female self – normally suppressed – emerge? Or does it mean the very opposite: that only when in male clothes can the male, or at least bisexual, figure deep down inside her fully and secretly live itself? It is these questions which the whole political, sexual, and political/sexual argument hangs round.

The evidence from within the play has to be listed briefly. Rubinstein (1984) states: 'in *As You Like It*, as the title itself may have been intended to communicate, a feeling of bisexuality pervades the whole play' (p. 358). Rosalind takes for herself the name 'Ganymede': catamite; male prostitute. She is 'more than common tall', comes to life at the thought of wearing men's clothes, more than once puns on 'suit', and, of course, does wear male attire for most of the play's duration. Finally there is the brief suggestion of her relationship with Celia as 'dearer than the natural bond of sisters' (1, ii, 266). According to the Northrop Frye theory, comedy regenerates because the women imply the power of nurture; yet Rosalind (like most Shakespearian characters, it must be said) has no mother, and is contemptuous of 'ill-favoured children', the only reference she makes in the play to children apart from the admittedly ambiguous joke about her 'child's father', i.e. Orlando, at 1, iii, 11. (Some traditional editors reversed those two words; Norman Holland (1964) cited but questioned the view that it was a Freudian slip.)

There is another curious line on androgyny because of the play's historical position. In the seventeenth century, when Ganymede was on stage, a boy played a boy. Rainolds thought this 'monstrous', but in fact our actor Basil could, if he liked, mentally leave the woman bit out and just do Ganymede. By contrast, when a contemporary actress plays Moira she too, if she chooses, can, in her inner sense of the part, omit the male dimension of Ganymede altogether. And yet it is still the same part! It is Shakespeare's Rosalind from *As You Like It*. One could hardly have a more comprehensive illustration of the seamless stretch from female to male and back which this part provides. It does so uniquely, of course, because in no other play does the woman disguised as male then play back herself as woman too.

My suggestion is not that Rosalind is bisexual, less still lesbian, in some crude direct sense. Rather, Shakespeare has written into her that androgynous dimension, those signals, at least to a degree, and this attractive etherealised part, person or character alone can thus give a male–female reconciliation as deep as that of sacramental marriage. The latter implies separate genders; the androgynous is already a unity. Dusinberre shows (1975, pp. 200, 243, 251) that Erasmus, George Meredith and Virginia Woolf all moved, if varyingly, toward the idea of the androgynous as prototype of the adult mind, which rises above gender difference. Rosalind's spells thus work to inculcate this sense of union to the point where marriage may be seen as one (though perfectly valid and satisfying) form of it. It comes at the end, if at all. And since her spells are poetry itself, this secret is the secret of the play's unity, its undifferentiated, even if unusual, harmonies.

· 4 ·

Poetry

There are remarkable things to be found in *As You Like It*. For example, Rosalind's famous sad reply to Orlando, 'Say a day, without the ever' (IV, i, 138). Did Shakespeare know he had used all five vowels, and with such symmetrical elegance that the first two, appearing three times each, neatly surround the remaining three in correct order within: a-a-a i-o-u e-e-e? One suspects not but, thinking of the o's in a line like 'soft you, a word or two before you go' from *Othello*, one can hardly swear to it. Or the bawdy spoonerism available at III, ii, 129 if the b and s are swapped around in 'Buckles in his sum of age'? Then there are the many variants on the Welsh alliterative principle *cynghanedd*, as in 'a many merry men' (I, i, 115), 'the bountiful blind woman doth most mistake' (I, ii, 34) or 'the whetstone of the wits' (I, ii, 53). (Shakespeare may have ransacked Welsh for a time; his interest in Welsh characters is found in the recent Falstaff plays and *Henry V* which probably followed straight after *As You Like It*, while the weird word 'ducdame' here at II, v, 55 is Welsh for 'come to me', which fits.) There is the word 'fleet' in 'fleet the time carelessly' at I, i, 118, which seems in one fleeting glimpse to evoke fleet of ships, float, flaunt, flower, flourish, flee, flit and more.

These examples show perhaps that Shakespeare's renowned sweetness and eloquence are more than the enriched vocabulary of the Renaissance and the skill gained from professional experience when he had written nearly twenty plays. It is also letters, the very letters that make up the words. Shakespeare's suppleness of language arises from practised sensitivity to letter-placement at all levels and deft use of the results, like a David Gower who can flick the willow carelessly in sending the ball round the field in any direction according to occasion. By letter-placement 'at all levels' I am suggesting that it is more than the commonly used alliteration and pun, unusually easy and reposeful as they are. Rather, it is perpetual sensitivity to singles, pairs and trios of letters, how they hint at other words' meanings, or further half-heard meanings in themselves. (Consider, as just one example, the common O, L and R in 'Orlando' and 'Oliver'.) This extra dimension could then be combined with sensitivity to grammar, vocabulary and the intending imagined human speaker as well, into almost infinite possibilities. The trees are talking right across the forest, and every leaf matters. Hence – and in *As You Like It* more than anywhere – comes the exact sense of balance, of what passage to place where, what kind of indirection to use, to just the right degree of subtlety, how long to go on, what to leave unsaid, what hints to plant or leave planted, when vocabulary itself was so rich and the growing humanism of the day allowed patterns of thought and feeling to proliferate and diversify, as texts from the time aver. It is non-confrontational, fluent, murmuring, uncombative. One has only to look at the tunnel-vision elegance of Lyly and Lodge to see what was achieved.

From such perspective one can see how Rosalind's curving and arcing sentences grow. They are unique to her in the play, and they come when letters intertwine with words, phrases and feelings in huge and colourful elongations reminiscent of those twining models of molecular chains seen in chemistry laboratories. Early in Arden, on Orlando's dud poems she yawns:

Ay, but the feet were lame, and could not bear themselves without the verse, and therefore stood lamely in the verse.

(III, ii, 165–7)

Feeble pun, and a little lame certainly. But how the metre stirs at once – her very first words – when the man himself comes on the scene:

> Then there is no true lover in the forest, else sighing every minute and groaning every hour would detect the lazy foot of Time, as well as a clock.
>
> (III, ii, 297–9)

One could do a detailed analysis of these vowels and consonants. Note how the three grouped s's are distanced from 'lazy' by 'sighing and groaning', themselves split apart, and all following the meticulous balance of the vowels in the first nine words. Then comes the climax, or one of them:

Orlando Then in mine own person, I die.

Rosalind No, faith, die by attorney. The poor world is almost six thousand years old, and in all this time there was not any man died in his own person, videlicet, in a love-cause. Troilus had his brains dashed out with a Grecian club, yet he did what he could to die before, and he is one of the patterns of love. Leander, he would have lived many a fair year though Hero had turned nun, if it had not been for a hot mid summer night; for, good youth, he went but forth to wash him in the Hellespont, and being taken with the cramp, was drowned, and the foolish chroniclers of that age found it was Hero of Sestos. But these are all lies: men have died from time to time and worms have eaten them, but not for love.

> (IV, i, 89–103)

To call this merely alliteration or assonance would be to make it clay. There is a whispering *cynghanedd* in 'he did what he could to die', and the sequence '. . . love. Leander, he would have lived many a fair year' has subtleties of echo and expansion which readers can only respond to and associate with the play's human meaning for themselves. 'Turned nun', 'cramp,

was drowned', 'time and worms have eaten them'; to extract
them of course removes them from their place in the whole,
gently moving network of points where letter, word and
phrase coincide. As a single and no doubt arid exercise one
might trace the f and v sounds right through the passage, and
see what touches what. The passage swims and melts through
such connections.

But the same deployment of letters brings a challenging note
at the end: '. . . Sestos. But these are all lies . . .' To hear the
serpent's hiss might be extravagant; rather, where is the lying?
What are 'these'? If the letters and other language forms are
inextricable, as we have said, is this the poetry that is most
feigning? The debate on poetry as lies had highlighted the
literary talk of the years following Sidney's *Apologie for
Poetrie* (published 1595), which had answered the diatribe of
the disapproving Gosson – opponent of Lodge, too – in his
School of Abuse. Shakespeare was already working on at least
parts of *As You Like It* by this time. The subject becomes
pressing.

Truth and lies

For unfortunately, as said earlier, Rosalind's sigh that 'there is
no lover in the forest' simply isn't true; indeed, it is manipula-
tively untrue. If we then look to Touchstone's famous words
to Audrey as a possible key – 'The truest poetry is the most
feigning' – we find that too is ambiguous, for what does 'truest'
mean? It could either mean poetry that most tells the truth, or
that which is most poetical. And Touchstone proceeds to compromise the very word. For he had just told Audrey, 'Truly, I
would the gods had made thee poetical', and of that strange
new term Audrey asks, 'Is it a true thing?' To which Touchstone replies, 'No *truly*, for the truest poetry is the most
feigning' (my emphasis), and his next two speeches begin in
like kind: 'I do truly', 'No truly'. Not easy to trust, after that,
in what is after all a poetic drama if ever there was.

We get hardly more help at the end. There come what might
have been the play's clear resolving statements, from Orlando
and Duke Senior right at the end when Rosalind reveals who

she really is. 'If there be truth in sight, you are my daughter./ If there be truth in sight, you are my Rosalind' (v, iv, 117–18). Whose eyesight is named? Might they not mean the changed look in Rosalind's eye, that telling piece of body-language the Elizabethans valued so much, and which had subtly altered in Ganymede's form? The crunch comes a few lines later, with 'If truth holds true contents' in Hymen's hymn. As Malcolm Evans (1986) points out, despite its claim to 'bar confusion', this actually yields a permutation of 168 possible readings. Evans's absorbing game is somewhat over-the-top mathematically, yet he does unearth several convincing meanings for the line on the way, along with the presumed and obvious ones.

We sense from all this both the play's writerliness and the declaration of critics from Sir Philip Sidney to Paul de Man that all language by its very nature is capable of uttering more and less than it might seem. That is to say, it is capable of pluralising, shimmering, and indeed lying; and it is only poetry that is most honest because it acknowledges itself as fiction in the very act of flaunting how its words are separate from its supposed meanings. Yet that is hardly satisfactory, certainly not here. A play devoted to seamless and, on the whole, unthreatened love, and couched in such swimmingly delectable terms as well, might seem (again, as ever, Touchstone is speaking) 'to have honey a sauce to sugar' (III, iii, 26–7). Once more, perhaps, we recall the sugared sonnets. This text runs as sweet as honey. Even Duke Senior's firm statement on the rigours of nature surrounds 'the toad, ugly and venomous' with matching niceties, sweet in its uses of adversity, and sweetly alliterated (also, it happens, with *cynghanedd* variants):

> . . . tongues in trees, books in the running brooks,
> Sermons in stones, and good in everything.
>   (II, i, 16–17)

How can we rough up the text a bit? Sidney's defence allowed so-called 'lies' because they were really innocent: 'the poet nothing affirmes, and therefore never lyeth'. He also argued that the poet's freedom was to teach by delighting through 'what may be or should be' rather than what is.

(Shakespeare conceivably met Sidney, who died in battle at the age of 32 when the playwright was 22, and whose excellent and cultivated sister Mary had the two sons who were dedicatees of Shakespeare's 1623 folio.) Yet a sharper edge might seem to come from Bacon's scepticism:

> One of the later school of the Grecians [was unsure] what should be in it, that men should love lies; where neither they make for pleasure, as with poets; nor for advantage, as with the merchant; but for the lie's sake. But I cannot tell: this same truth is a naked and open day-light, that doth not shew the masques and mummeries and triumphs of the world, half so stately and daintily as candle-lights . . . A mixture of a lie doth ever add pleasure. ('Of Truth', p. 3)

The suggestion is that the 'poetry' in the play cannot and doesn't want to disentangle itself from the 'lies' of its own making, quite aside from the formal 'lie' that is fiction, which makes the overall narrative and imaginary story in the first place. The lie is of the disguise, which modifies everything that is said and makes the very language itself transvestite. Puns are transvestite. Puns and alliteration always offer two verbal genders, so to speak, in the same statement; always providing indistinct slippage and no sharp edge from one phrase to the next. Touchstone's computation of the seven kinds of lie toward the end make a jest of the very idea of lie and truth; and 'truth' itself, as in his own statement cited above, is very slippery indeed. Yet to contrast beauty and honesty in terms of poetry – poetry and prose now, rather than honey and sugar – would be too crude, even if as with Audrey it works for country wenches, whose husbands have a position to guard. It is too tenuous, too hypothetical, too iffy indeed, and the virtue in 'If' is what Touchstone himself finally lighted on. For by then he had demolished lies too (v, iv, 67–102). Indeed, by hilarious juxtaposition, the idea that the ample Audrey might 'bear her body more seemly' was 'a lie seven times removed'.

If

The word 'if' occurs 133 times in the play. Its prominence has often been noted (Young, 1972, Lifson, 1987, *et al.*). The whole 'just suppose' tradition of earlier comedy exemplified by Ariosto's fifteenth-century comedy *Suppositi*, embodies the artifices, deceits and exchanges which comedy uses to explore all the possibilities of human ramification. Gascoigne's adaptation of Ariosto's play as *Supposes* was performed at Gray's Inn in 1566; it may have been known to Shakespeare later.

We can calculate the varying frequency of these 133 Ifs. It is quite interesting. The following table scans their frequency in a number of ways (we might as well enjoy the sense of numerate knowledge that statistics offer):

	Lines	Ifs	Ifs per 100 lines	No. of lines per If
Act I	584	30	5.1	19.5
Act II	544	31	5.7	17.5
Act III	733	20	2.7	36.6
Act IV	409	11	2.7	37.2
Act V	452	41	9.1	11.0

Whatever we make of this, it is very clear statistically. If Act I is our 'standard rate' of Ifs, Act II is the same, Acts III and IV halve it, and Act V doubles it. And, apart from the slight discrepancy between Acts I and II, the tidiness of the overall finding is remarkable. Figures for Acts III and IV are identical, and, when calculated as 'lines per If', the figures for Acts III and IV are almost *exactly* double those for Act I. (That is to say, the frequency of Ifs per line in Act I is almost *exactly* double that in Acts III and IV.) Act V's Ifs are not *exactly* double those of Act I, but they aren't far off.

But there is another remarkable If-feature in the play. That is the frequency with which they appear in twos or even threes. This paralleling usually occurs at the beginnings of lines whether prose or verse. Of the 133 Ifs in the play, only a quarter stand alone. This becomes overwhelming in the final act, where virtually none is alone. As with so many of the letter-effects one sees throughout the text, one may not imagine

Shakespeare plotting them in consciously (though I would so like to have seen his notebooks, line-blotted or not), but they come deftly from his practised skill over decades, and he was surely aware they were there.

'If' in our language has gentle shades of grey above and below the mean of pure hypothesis: if this is so, that is so. For it can also be weakened or pessimistic, as in an if-but-only-if emphasis: 'if it's a really hot day then perhaps we'll go; otherwise not'. And equally it can be positive and challenging in the strong form: if X, then most certainly Y: 'Watch it. If you go too near you'll burn yourself.' These shades of meaning come and go in *As You Like It*. Most readers, one imagines, would have intuited the dominance of this word in the fifth act. All kinds of evocations and possibilities are suggested, mainly by Rosalind; indeed it is the backbone language of her spells, which she then reaffirms when all is made even at the end. What is surprising, perhaps, is the frequency, though less so, in Act I.

In Act I the tenor of the if-passages is threat, and response to threat. This is the 'if X, then certainly Y' kind. It begins, appropriately enough, with Charles the wrestler: 'If he come tomorrow, I'll give him his payment [i.e. beat him up for his treachery]. If ever he go alone again, I'll never wrestle for prize more' (I, i, 157–9). This pair seems to be answered by Orlando's resigned attitude before the bout: 'if I be foiled, there is but one shamed that was never gracious; if killed, but one dead that is willing to be so' (I, ii, 176–8). In between, in the only other if-pairings so early, Touchstone (one of the play's most frequent iffers) jokes about honour and its lack: 'By my knavery, if I had it, then I were [a knave]. But if you swear by that that is not, you are not foresworn. No more was this knight . . . or if he had, he had sworn it away before ever he saw those pancakes or that mustard' (I, ii, 70–4).

These passages re-echo when the play's one political event occurs, at the end of Act I:

Duke Frederick   You cousin.
   Within these ten days if that thou be'st found
   So near our public court as twenty miles,
   Thou diest for it.

> *Rosalind*   I do beseech your grace,
> Let me the knowledge of my fault bear with me.
> If with myself I hold intelligence,
> Or have acquaintance with mine own desires,
> If that I do not dream, or be not frantic,
> As I do trust I am not, then dear uncle,
> Never so much as in a thought unborn
> Did I offend your Highness.
> *Duke Frederick*   Thus do all traitors.
> If their purgation did consist in words,
> They are as innocent as grace itself.
>
> (I, iii, 38–50)

There are grades of the conditional here (particularly in the
Duke's two uses) which diversify in the next two acts. Threat
of one kind or another follows: from Touchstone rather bully-
ingly to Corin (III, ii, 39–40) and from the waspish Phebe
to Silvius (III, v, 16–18), still coming in pairs. But one who
continues to talk this way is Orlando, and now the threats are
felt from nature. In finding food for Adam, and cheering him
up, it seems entirely whimsical: 'If this uncouth forest yield
anything savage, I will either be food for it, or bring it for food
to thee . . . If I bring thee not something to eat, I will give thee
leave to die; but if thou diest before I come, thou art a mocker
of my labour . . . Thou shalt not die for lack of a dinner, if there
live any thing in this desert' (II, vi, 6–7, 11–13, 16–17). His
determination to help and cheer the old man seems tied to this
hypothetic stance, which could be read as either a precaution-
ary cover for himself, or renewed will-power. To Duke Senior
Orlando then becomes very emphatic, but in the same terms
grammatically:

> If ever you have look'd on better days;
> If ever been where bells have knoll'd to church;
> If ever sat at any good man's feast;
> If ever from your eyelids wip'd a tear

– then have pity and feed us (II, vii, 113–16).
    In the next two acts If is less frequent but still present. It
becomes song-like in Silvius's strain to Corin, sardonic in

Jaques and Touchstone at II, v, 47–54 and III, ii, 99, 101. Rosalind is scathing about Silvius's weak-kneed wooing just before Oliver arrives (IV, iii, 70–4):

> . . . say this to her: that if she love me, I charge her to love thee. If she will not, I will never have her, unless thou entreat for her. If you be a true lover, hence, and not a word; for here comes more company.

It is as though everything must be left tentative and whimsical even when life itself is at stake, and regardless of emotional context, from threat to jocular philosophy to promise. The fifth act yields up a torrent of Ifs: as it has been put, If becomes the play's protagonist. At least they fall into clear passages. Phebe, Silvius and Orlando ask defiantly of their loves, what blame is there if the Pauline love Silvius intones is real? At once Rosalind puts her conditional and qualified promises all round (v, ii, 111–22). The next day, she reminds them all of their sides of those bargains:

Rosalind	You say, if I bring in your Rosalind, You will bestow her on Orlando here?
Duke Senior	That would I, had I kingdoms to give with her.
Rosalind	And you say you will have her, when I bring her?
Orlando	That would I, were I of all kingdoms king.
Rosalind	You say you'll marry me, if I be willing?
Phebe	That will I, should I die the hour after.
Rosalind	But if you do refuse to marry me, You'll give yourself to this most faithful shepherd?
Phebe	So is the bargain.
Rosalind	You say that you'll have Phebe if she will?
Silvius	Though to have her and death were both one thing.
Rosalind	I have promis'd to make all this matter even.

(v, iv, 6–18)

The Duke, Orlando and Phebe all seem curiously reluctant to utter the word here, while keeping the substance. After

Touchstone's extraordinarily reassuring discourse on the seven lies, with 'If' – 'much virtue in If' – as the way to avoid that sad recourse, Hymen enters with Rosalind and Celia restored to their own selves. The act of 'making all things even' becomes a levelling or reduction, in a pre-scientific world, to homogeneity. The Renaissance analogical understanding of reality, the deep sense that everything is microcosm of a larger world-pattern, allows in this endlessly conditional, open presentation of possibilities of language, poetry, fiction, love, nature and power too. But this occurs in a world of expansion and change. Fortune is capricious, humans are no longer at the universe's centre, and divinity of kings and solitary eminence even of the old world gives way before the voyages of discovery to the Americas.

The startling implication comes in Hymen's final verse when the spate of Ifs has subsided:

> Peace ho! I bar confusion.
> 'Tis I must make conclusion
>   Of these most strange events

– and we recall that this 'strange eventful history' is what Jaques had termed human life itself in its seven ages, of which this play has been just a part. Life's 'events' are its relationships, its small transformations and misunderstandings leading to enlargings, and themselves in turn thwarted, or still left open, after the epilogue itself. 'If' is itself the basis of a poetry; it allows any humanity, any language, yet because always conditional, it is never violent, is gentleness itself.

There is no 'if' in Jaques's 'seven ages' speech. For that matter, Celia never says the word either. Only Touchstone, perhaps, combined detachment and perception enough to avoid committing himself other than to his straightforward desires. But at the price such detachment has to take.

· 5 ·

Touchstone and folly

Touchstone does very little. Apart from picking up an unchallenging country girl, he merely follows Rosalind and Celia and lounges on the forest floor with his laconic speculations. He is thus no conventional trickster, despite being more the part for that than is Jaques. He plays no practical jokes, sets no traps, hides in no corners, gets no one drunk, brings no false tidings. Tricksters had begun to seem boorish to the well-rounded courtiers and humanistically educated Elizabethans in the audience. But there are three passages where Touchstone bullies: to the unimpressed yet defenceless Corin, to Audrey herself and, wholly redundantly, to Audrey's erstwhile boyfriend William, who enters the play for only enough time to be seen off by Touchstone's line in comic sub-plot banishment. Perhaps, as has been suggested by some, the old rustic clown is being displaced by the new court one, for Touchstone is new in English drama.

Salingar (1974, p. 293) argued, like Jenkins (1967), that *As You Like It* is typified by characters who walk on when others are speaking, and intrude with comments on their conversation. Rosalind, Jaques and indeed Oliver all do this, and in a sense Phebe too. But Touchstone does not. Touchstone is the one who can knowingly spot and avoid folly without going much further. He covers himself, takes no risky action which would expose him, and eventually has 'if' the first and last word of his main speech (v, iv, 43–102). Touchstone's comments are not *ad hominem* or *ad feminam*. Jaques aims high in the intellectual stakes, and makes it perhaps, but at cost to his own power of commanding respect; his reflections are always ahead of his poise. Touchstone succeeds, but by aiming lower. For this reason Jaques is intrigued by him, and summarises him him perhaps adequately:

> . . . in his brain,
> Which is as dry as the remainder biscuit
> After a voyage, he hath strange places cramm'd
> With observation, the which he vents
> In mangled forms.
>
> (II, vii, 38–42)

Touchstone, in short, is Jaques's foil.

From this distinction between Jaques and Touchstone we can see how the Nature–Wit–Folly–Fortune argument spreads through the play more widely. As John Lyly had said, one gets wit by nature. But the fuller source here is Erasmus. The witty person sees that life is no fun without pleasure, and so folly too; and also that to succeed while foolish one needs a little fortune along the way. So while wit is evidently superior, folly must be indulged and enjoyed in oneself and others. Touchstone has this level of understanding, but never develops it.

Erasmus's line further, in *In Praise of Folly*, was that since folly is everywhere, and since a large part of pleasure, which everyone wants, is knowingly folly, then those who claim to be wholly wise are merely labelling themselves foolish all the more. Touchstone would appear to embody this attitude – he virtually quotes it at v, i, 30–1 – and for that very reason frees Jaques, who cannot get outside his own inner wrestlings, still to say substantial things too. Jaques would at least struggle with the 'foul contagion of the world', perhaps aware too that such 'ill-favoured' qualities (one of the play's key terms) are of Nature (another): Audrey can't be other than she is. Touchstone takes her for sheer carnal satisfaction (III, iii, 71); he is not a full player on the stage. What Jaques painfully works out and says, Touchstone knows.

But equally, by watching without intervening, Touchstone seems to approve the attitude that Jaques's main speech expresses. Erasmus had said it in the same work: 'What else is the whole life of man but a sort of play? Actors come on wearing their different masks and all play their parts until the producer orders them off the stage' (1971, p. 104). The metaphor of human life as a stage was apparently very necessary to the sixteenth century for explanatory reasons, and it recurs often. But the audience just watches, and for the actors to survive at all they must have fortune, to a degree, on their side. As Touchstone says – quoted by Jaques – 'call me not fool, till heaven hath sent me fortune' (II, vii, 19). Touchstone is suspiciously close at times to affecting knowledge of wisdom and wit while not developing them beyond the objective, parasitical comment. 'Thus men may grow wiser every day. It is the first time that ever I heard breaking of ribs was sport for ladies' (I, ii, 127–9). Yet the innocent Le Beau was only doing his job.

Salingar suggested that, on procuring Robert Armin to the Chamberlain's company, Shakespeare began to generate fools who were 'wise men wearing camouflage' (1974, p. 246), and Felver argued (Lathem, 1975, p. lxvii) that Armin was himself the source for Touchstone. But, in this play more than most, Touchstone can't be sole holder of this role. This is one of the play's deepest ambiguities. For Erasmus's Folly-figure was a woman. In his book she speaks in her own voice, saying, 'if the philosopher ever wants to be a father it's me he has to call on – yes, me' (1971, p. 76). Wisdom and certainly worldly prudence (of a traditionally male kind) must be touched with folly-pleasure in order to generate. So Rosalind it is whose language seems to inscribe judgement with emotion and love, but laughing at her own folly for doing so. Erasmus's Folly derides those who work at tomes for years and affect spontaneity, whereas she herself 'always liked best to say whatever was on the tip of my tongue' (p. 66), a remark pre-echoing Rosalind's own: 'Do you not know I am a woman? When I think, I must speak' (III, ii, 245–6). Yet Touchstone, not Rosalind (despite I, iii, 11), would seem more likely to engender children, to procreate.

Touchstone seemingly knows what poetry is, even that it is 'feigning'. His talk embodies both the wisdom and limitation that must 'let the forest judge' (III, ii, 119). Rosalind, by contrast, speaks the very poetry itself.

Indeed, *In Praise of Folly* seems more to pervade the play the more one considers it. Erasmus's folly declares that truth must be touched with pleasure, that dissembling is an essential skill, that there are 'wise fools', that fools are much loved by women, and even – tying Silvius to St Paul again – that God's folly of charity is wiser than men's wisdom. Erasmus's list of the questionably wise has a little of the sardony found in Jaques's examples of the seven ages. In fact *As You Like It* seems to split Erasmus's Folly-figure between Jaques and Touchstone fairly equably, so that it is the wider spirit pervading that counts. And unlike Erasmus's even-paced satire, Shakespeare's patchwork atmosphere seems to end up on no particular side while raising all of them. Touchstone's name may imply, as often suggested, that such considerations always pass through the switchboard of himself, but they do not rest there.

Oliver and Celia

But then, after more than two acts of idle talking, wooing and differentiated and undifferentiated gender, there is very suddenly Oliver's later appearance in the forest.

Oliver brings news, a story, a rescue, blood. He stops the talk, focuses Celia, and with his abrupt conversion restores the moral as that which challenges rather than merely defines or ponders. In so doing he throws into sharp black-and-white many issues which have been lurking and drifting with decreasing focus: love, poetry, good-and-evil, friendship itself. If wisdom and wooing have absorbed us as these intricacies suggest, Oliver's entrance – despite his own new gentleness – is sharp and violent indeed.

After three Ifs of his own in his first four speeches, Oliver suddenly turns Greek messenger. He tells an extraordinary story, almost a mini-epic or proto-*Paradise Lost* in barely fifty lines. It is complete with lioness and snake, a brave hero nearly killed to save his brother and (perhaps) impress his lady, and the defeat of an evil man bent on revenge by a force of primal and mythic goodness. The blood on the napkin is tinged with the sacramental. It has no detail, it is three times simply 'this bloody napkin', 'this napkin, dy'd in his blood', the only addition being the elemental animal cause, that the lioness 'had torn some flesh away'. Orlando is not wounded in Lodge's version, and it is as though here the lioness provides the deer's revenge. All of this occurs 'under an old oak', in which Christian and Edenesque tree of knowledge seem to be enwrapped, and of prehistoric implication, 'high bald top with dry antiquity'.

Furthermore of course, Oliver is himself wrapped into his own story. It was he who had the play's only real soliloquy, right back at I, i, 161–71, where the oft-remarked foreshadowing of Iago, while certainly there, surely prefigures Milton's Satan too. Satan wrestles with the inherent contradictions that evil's ignorance entails in him. Says Oliver: 'My soul – yet I know not why – hates nothing more than he. Yet he's gentle, never schooled, yet learned, full of noble device . . . so much in the heart of the world . . . that I am altogether misprised' (I, i, 163–9). In Act IV, Oliver's escape from this misprision in a single line – ''Twas I. But 'tis not I' – goes on when he states that 'my conversion so sweetly tastes, being the thing I am'. If the lioness has revenged the deer, Oliver has defeated his own earlier self. This encapsulation of the medieval *felix culpa* and blissful acknowledgement of sin with the Cartesian *cogito* hits play, characters and audience on several levels at once. For the sharp contrast of the two Olivers seems to match the gender difference which Rosalind and Orlando had increasingly obscured. Heterosexual lovers like Oliver and Celia can't merge imperceptibly into one another, they have to go at it 'in the very wrath of love; clubs cannot part them' so hard do they strive against the obdurate barriers of the sexed flesh.

Oliver's story is at one with its mode of long-speech, blank-verse narrative. As such it seems almost wilfully to line up with Jaques's speeches (the seven ages one but not only that), as third in the trio underlined by Sidney as the modes of human understanding among which poetry was superior. Oliver's speech is historical (it gives examples, but only actual ones) and Jaques's is philosophical (giving precepts, but not actual instances). Poetry can do both. The multi-layered texture of this play's writing seems to offer that poetry can encapsulate the other two, can delight, and instruct by delighting, by not staying rigidly within the hard boundaries of intellectual disciplines. Oliver's dark and mythological mode of expressing story, blank verse line and personal conversion, all insert a change into the play's previous honeyed movement which is irreversible.

It also raises the question – asked over the centuries, as we saw – of the Oliver–Celia match and how it is justified. If you are a Bradleian, the change in Oliver also hits Celia, who had perhaps experienced a slow, unnoticed about-turn in her relations with Rosalind. In all this forest-talk Celia had said little: in Act v she says not one word. She meets a man who equally avoids dialogue, but from the opposite alternative of extended narration. The wider question Shakespeare is raising seems to be that of friendship itself, and what subverts it. My suggestion, in now attending to Celia, is that Shakespeare may have been deliberately pitching up the Rosalind–Celia friendship as a female counterpart, to see what might become of it.

The long-established friendship literature was hitherto largely male. Aristotle and Plato had both affirmed male friendship as a superior order of human love to male–female relationship. Montaigne saw friendship as the best form of society, superior even to brotherhood and paternal–filial bonds. It is highly likely that Shakespeare had in mind both Chaucer's *Knight's Tale* but also John Lyly's *Euphues* when writing his own friendship story in *Two Gentlemen of Verona*, in which Proteus is led away from his friendship bond with Valentine by desire for Valentine's lady-love Silvia (= 'woodland girl'). Proteus's own earlier heart-throb was Julia, precursor of Rosalind in that she adopted male disguise. But there also seems to be an echo of *Euphues* in *As You Like It*. Celia protests her friendship with Rosalind to Duke Frederick, to prevent Rosalind's banishment:

> We still have slept together,
> Rose at an instant, learn'd, play'd, eat together,
> And whereso'er we went, like Juno's swans,
> Still we went coupled and inseparable.
>
> (I, iii, 69–72)

This is close to the male friendship of Euphues and Philautus in Lyly's story: 'they vsed not only one boord, but one bedde, one booke . . . their friendship augmented euery day, insomuch yt the one could not refraine ye companie of ye other one minute, all things went in comon betweene them, which all men accompted comendable' (1902, vol. 1, p. 199).

By the nature of the case the lesbian dimension in the play becomes possible, following almost inevitably with the androgynous. Of course, it needn't follow: as Sarah Jeffreys wrote, 'In the eighteenth and nineteenth centuries many middle class women had relations with each other which included passionate declarations of love, nights spent in bed together sharing kisses and intimacies, and lifelong devotion, without exciting the least adverse comment' (in Kitzinger, 1987, ch. 2). It is a strand of implication which can be taken many ways. What matters is the relationship, as that is presented, between Rosalind and Celia, and what it does with the language and that in turn with it. Celia claims the friendship three times in Act I: I, iii, 69 here, again at 92ff. but also earlier in almost her part's first words, with its grave monosyllables: 'Herein I see thou lov'st me not with the full weight that I love thee'. Rosalind never reciprocates, and while her curving flights of language grow Celia is contrastingly terse and monotone, on Orlando as much as anything else: 'O wonderful, wonderful! And most wonderful wonderful! And yet again wonderful! And after that out of all whooping' (III, ii, 188–90). Celia's remark that she does 'not hate' Orlando has uncomfortably ambivalent resonance.

But, finally, Celia ends the whole wooing charade with a dejected 'And I'll sleep'. But that is what Oliver is doing, when Orlando finds him – the 'sleeping man' (IV, iii, 116). And this is a marked parallel to Rosalind's response to the 'fainting man' Orlando (IV, iii, 148, 149), that she herself faints. We are thus given the clinching detail that Celia's match, in the four-square world of comic doubles, is at last found. It is this kind of argument that seems to me to answer the doubts, over two centuries, as to the propriety and likelihood of the Celia–Oliver match.

Comic duality: Silvius, Phebe, Corin and Jaques de Boys

There is an equal robustness and clarity about the pairing of
Silvius and Phebe, as against that of Orlando and Rosalind, just
as there is of Oliver and Celia against the same pair, although
the Silvius/Phebe match is briefer in presentation. And, of
course, the early meeting with Silvius (II, iv, 17ff.) sets him up
as parody against which Orlando the hero can to some extent
be favourably contrasted.

But one aspect of this underplot is not often mentioned. It is
that Silvius's first comic pairing-and-contrast, his own point of
balance in the play, is not Phebe but Corin. We tend to recall
the play as containing four pairs of lovers, with the Silvius–
Phebe match containing the contrast of a blind, love-sick swain
with a scornful and somewhat cunning shepherd-girl. But this
comes later. The first contrast, from the moment they enter, is
between Silvius's young, wordy, ignorant but too confident
misery, and Corin's old, terse, experienced and more detached
equanimity:

Silvius	No Corin, being old, thou canst not guess,
	Though in thy youth thou wast as true a lover
	As ever sigh'd upon a midnight pillow.
	But if thy love were ever like to mine,
	As sure I think did never man love so,
	How many actions most ridiculous
	Hast thou been drawn to by thy fantasy?
Corin	Into a thousand that I have forgotten.
Silvius	O thou didst then never love so heartily.
	If thou remember'st not the slightest folly
	That ever love did make thee run into,
	Thou hast not lov'd.
	Or if thou hast not sat as I do now,
	Wearying thy hearer in thy mistress' praise,
	Thou hast not lov'd.
	Or if thou hast not broke from company . . .

(II, iv, 22–37)

Silvius's whole thrust – to get pity, to be sure – is to contrast
Corin with himself. The ludicrous nature of his words

depends on the presence of the different listener who can see the obverse side. What is then remarkable is that Rosalind herself – who has just pointed up this contrast in a single line, 'A young man and an old in solemn talk' – then introduces her own note, different again, this time by its wistfulness:

> Alas, poor shepherd, searching of thy wound,
> I have by hard adventure found mine own.

But Touchstone immediately takes the theme into a further dimension still, the greasy bawdiness of his own amorous recollections with Jane Smile. This contrasts not only Silvius but Corin too. The all-important theme of comic duality is thus being brought in here economically and at an early stage; Silvius has no power to attract us into any inner individualist soul, and his claim to that is made absurd. Phebe's forthcoming lack of interest in him is thus easy to take. Perhaps this character more than any in the play takes us back to Lodge: 'Montanus ended his sonnet with such a volley of sighs, and such a streame of tears, as might have moved any but Phoebe to have granted him favor' (1902, p. 134).

So when Phebe enters we already know where she belongs. This allows her love-play for Ganymede to pierce via her black eyes rather than from the play's heart. But she survives comic collapse, because of a cunning duality of her own. In the height and depth of her supposed love for Ganymede she still contrives a judicious balance on the tight-rope:

> Think not I love him, though I ask for him.
> 'Tis but a peevish boy – yet he talks well –
> But what care I for words? Yet words do well
> When he that speaks them pleases those that hear.
> It is a pretty youth – not very pretty –
> But sure he's proud, and yet his pride becomes him . . .
> He is not very tall, yet for his years he's tall.
> His leg is but so so, and yet 'tis well . . .
>
> (III, v, 109–14, 118–19)

Duality is itself redoubled, for in this elegantly schizoid speech Phebe seems to be controlling each phrase as she lets it out little by little. So she herself also presents, along with her inner self-known split, an exact opposite to Silvius's monotone sighings. Phebe's double-attitude at this point seems to imply her recognition of her double-position in the pattern of loves, and with deeper implications. For she is not only in tension between Silvius, whom she rejects and is wanted by, and Ganymede, whom she wants and is rejected by; she also matches and contrasts Orlando in their shared ignorance. Orlando can have Rosalind-Ganymede but doesn't know it; Phebe cannot, and equally doesn't know it. According to authority cited by Holland (1964, p. 156), this pattern matches one found for homosexuality in clinical practice. The relevant pattern, presumably, is that the two aspects of a bisexual person symbolised by Phebe and Orlando feel the two forces of outside convention as to what they may and may not sexually desire. Is it that by making comic something which controls one's life at both biological and social level, Shakespeare raises it into available consciousness? Perhaps by raising it he renders it comic.

The inherence of doubles in comedy is often remarked on, yet not often examined as a totality. But the pairings, twins, disguises of self as someone else, reversals of plan, juxtapositions of lord with peasant, fop with clown and so on, and post-music hall pairings too (Laurel and Hardy, Morecambe and Wise, Fry and Laurie, French and Saunders) provide a key for interpretation of much of comedy in its several embodiments. To see what, if it would command respect, ought to be the integration of a feeling and thinking character, now split in itself, provides the explosive element for laughter by having two meanings available at once for any situation. It also gives us, the audience, the necessary freedom from threat to our own self-estimate to allow the risk laughter would entail in real life.

The split is achieved by the difference between the real truth and the character's ignorant, wrong version of it; awkwardness in disguise between real self and part played; contrast between the lover who desires and is unrequited and the loved who wants none of it; the treatment of someone from our experience of them when it is really their twin; etc., etc. Obviously, a person can't enter a real situation fully if they are treated mistakenly as someone else, or haven't understood the situation; we the audience do understand it and have emotional relief by the nervous bark of the larynx which laughter is. But all of this no doubt routine summary of comic structure becomes more than usually important in *As You Like It*. There, the central character knows who she is despite her disguise, and also is not – unlike Viola – carrying out the disguise for a practical reason (concealment from fear, attempted burglary, etc.) which could backfire. Rosalind 'learns', we are frequently told, and she does, at that level, but rather it is that in plays like this a new level and kind of philosophical, imaginative comedy gets created. In Lyly's phrase, it is 'soft smiling not loud laughing'.

This is the concomitant of the lack of action with which we started. The play is loaded with pairs – two dukes, two brothers whose names begin with 'O', two female cousins, four love-matches, two intellectuals/clowns. But they don't trip over tree-roots or have to hide in bedroom closets; rather, the pairs generate further pairings. Rosalind/Celia and Orlando/Oliver become Rosalind/Orlando and Oliver/Celia; Phebe and Orlando pair in wanting Ganymede; Jaques/Touchstone pair, but so do Touchstone/Audrey. And so audience reaction and reader response get distended into a kind of contentment. And these pairings, furthermore, even extend to the very last character, Jaques de Boys, who enters in Act V just in time to go out again.

It is often said that this Jaques is further evidence of the play's unfinished nature, for Jaques de Boys is the missing Ferdinand from Lodge, 'thy middle brother, he is a scholler and hath no mind but on Aristotle: let him read on Galen while thou riflest with golde' (1902, p. 12). But, in cutting him, Shakespeare also craftily keeps him in, for he not only ends the play but also begins it. He is Orlando's very first sardonic memory in the very first lines of Act I: 'my brother Jaques he keeps at school, and report speaks goldenly of his profit'. Since 'he' is Oliver, who treats this Jaques far better than he treats Orlando, a question arises: whose side is Jaques de Boys on, when he rides in at the end? He might have been expected to run for the monastery too. (Jaques de Boys is also mentioned, very briefly, at II, ii, 18.)

An idle question, perhaps, but Jaques de Boys nicely fits the dual pattern. For even in name alone he contrasts the melancholic Jaques, so that Shakespeare – reversing the values in poker – has divided a threesome of brothers into two pairs. As Jaques/Jaques de Boys and Oliver/Orlando, they come complete with matching names. But Jaques de Boys also ends the tenuous discourse the play is made of. He finishes his account of Frederick's conversion and renunciation from warfare with the declaration: 'This to be true, I do engage my life'. Truth at last allows no argument. The ifs and perhapses disperse, and the comic dust settles. There is nothing to add; the final pairing is complete.

Mirth in heaven

And so to the end, and the four couples marry, presumably to live happily ever after.

> Then is there mirth in heaven,
> When earthly things made even
>   Atone together.
> Good Duke receive thy daughter,
> Hymen from heaven brought her,
>   Yea brought her hither,
> That thou mightst join her hand with his
> Whose heart within his bosom is.
>   (v, iv, 107–14)

So neat that all is made not odd (the shambles of knockabout comedy) but even (the well-ordered and reflective comedy of soft smiling not loud laughing). And yet – not so fast.

'Mirth'? Isn't that a little odd just now? Surely 'joy' would be more the word, and would fit the metre exactly. And why tell us that Orlando's 'heart within his bosom is'? Shouldn't that be 'hers'? Some editors amend, but the folio reading is clear enough. To a comparable truism in *Hamlet* Marcellus replies 'there needs no ghost come from the grave/ To tell us this'. Is somebody having one last joke?

The joke I have in mind has, as it happens, been going around these last few months: 'If you want to make God laugh, tell him your plans'. It is the restored Duke Senior, needless to say, who proceeds to tell God their plans at v, iv, 169–78 and again at 196–7. But no one actually does marry in the play itself. We may interpret it that they intend to, but that is different. The textual evidence is ambivalent. Hymen is the god of marriage, and so his song ('Wedding is great Juno's crown') might be conceived of as a wedding rite in itself. ('Hymen' was originally the name of the bridal song itself, but this became personified.) This appears supported by Phebe's remark to Silvius right after the song: '*now thou art mine,*/ Thy faith my fancy to thee doth combine' (my emphasis). But the Duke seems to think the weddings are still to come. At line 169 he says 'First, in this forest, let us do those ends/ That here were well begun and well begot'. Then even more pointedly, in the very last two lines of the play apart from the epilogue, he says 'We will *begin* these rites,/ As we do trust they'll end, in true delights' (my emphasis once more).

It depends then whether Hymen has already married them. Again it is ambivalent. The crucial words (v, iv, 127–9, again my emphasis) are:

Here's eight that *must* take hands
To join in Hymen's bands,
    If truth holds true contents.

If they 'must', they haven't yet. That 'if' again, seven times in the preceding ten lines, let alone a further ten in Touchstone's 'If' speech immediately before that. This line, 'If truth holds true contents', taken apart by Malcolm Evans (1986) into 168 different readings as said earlier, is truism embodied, compounding Hymen's 'must' and his predictions in the song's next few lines. It ends:

Whiles a wedlock hymn we sing
Feed yourselves with questioning,
That reason wonder may diminish
How thus we met, and these things finish.

How indeed, and 'questioning' will solve little unless we can tell whether 'reason' is subject and 'wonder' object or the reverse (for a similar subject–object confounding, cf. II, vii,

53). The final song that follows does no more than 'honour wedlock' in the most general terms.

To compound this last irony further, the play has of course already had two abortive 'marriages', one of dubious validity between Orlando and Rosalind, when Celia could not 'say the words', and one between Touchstone and Audrey under Sir Oliver Martext, which never happened. We recall too perhaps Rosalind's line 'say a day, without the ever', which starts one of her two lyrically wistful speeches, sad in their realism about marriage after the impulsive love which went before, and which, said C.L. Barber (1959, pp. 235–6), effectively end the play in that they indicate that an emotional climax has been reached. From then on the feeling winds down, perhaps to just a touch of despondency. And this 'say a day' may bring to mind Orlando's line when Rosalind reverts to female dress: 'If there be truth in sight, you are my Rosalind' (v, iv, 118). He never says another word. More than one critic has wondered about this, only the extreme case being Ralph Berry's question (1972, p. 184) as to what Orlando must be thinking on learning that 'his wife-to-be has been fooling him'. Orlando might equally be realising that his 'pretty youth' Ganymede is no more and that routine bourgeois marriage beckons. He has not seen the real Rosalind since the few brief minutes after the wrestling in Act 1, which was the first time in any case.

None of this is to deny another – indeed the usual – perfectly obvious and legitimate reading, that the four couples do indeed marry right after the play ends, and happily. Historians of the period such as Laslett, Wrightson and MacFarlane do not at all give a picture of marriage as merely brutal male domination in loveless pairings based on superstitious church belief and negotiation of land, money and dowries. A more moderate picture, authenticated, suggests a two-level relationship consisting of male authority in the marriage certainly, but that often operating at a formal, though real, level, with much mutual affection, understanding and emotional interdependence and support at the more intimate level. Diaries, wills and other evidence suggest that the so-called companionate marriage was well established by the sixteenth century, and that choice by young people of their marriage partners was quite free, even when officially parents could claim a say in the matter. Any barrier along those lines is demolished by Shakespeare in *As You Like It* at II, vii, 194–9, where Duke Senior recognises and welcomes Orlando in the most affectionate terms as son of the man he loved. The 'double standard' element is quite another matter, but is never raised as a crucial issue for the characters during the play itself, much as Rosalind may be expressing it in her 'die by attorney' and 'say a day' speeches. The songs deal with it as bawdy, but as we said at the start, there are no actual love rivalries.

Rather, the suggestion is that the play enables our own freedom of interpretation yet again. Writing of *As You Like It*, Docherty refers to 'the supposed final values of the play, marriage and the praise of a very specific kind of family' and names this as the 'nuclear family' (1987, pp. 101–2). One has to point out that dukes and their offspring would hardly have lived in nuclear families. And when he says the characters by the end have 'learnt precisely nothing. They simply corroborate an ideology which has caused their problems in the first place', I can only feel he has missed the joke. Rosalind certainly and Orlando perhaps have both questioned marriage markedly, and we don't know what comes of the result. As Salingar (1974) put it in Baconian fashion, we have been invited to enjoy a little deceit and some 'agreeable mistakes', because Fortune (not ideology) is the trickster who throws our systems askance. All we know is that Basil in the epilogue hopes both men and women in the audience have 'liked it', and that 'if he were a woman' he would kiss the ones he physically fancied. 'Farewell.' The comedy lasts till the last word.

· 6 ·

The Golden Age and time

So we look up, and see the wider arena where is acted out the play's overall theme and ambience.

If this view of the marriages is challenged as escapist, then any answer might begin with the wider escapism the whole play is often said to embody. Our suggestion in the previous section was, in effect, that rather than the marriages ending the play, the play ends the marriages. We are free to speculate whether they occurred only because Shakespeare chose to cut off the play when, seemingly, they were about to occur. That leaves them as a utopian and unexamined future, which can therefore be left as obverse dream to the Golden Age origin and setting conceived for Arden. The way that conceptions of time weave in and out of the text is clearly germane to this. They are, however, an enriching rather than explanatory theme; no neat analysis of them can be given.

Theories of time throw much useful light on this play. They appear in several disciplines: mathematical, anthropological, philosophical, cosmological or literary. Almost all arrive at some kind of two-tiered idea in which a current ongoing (or 'arrow') experience of time has a huge cataclysmic event at some point long prior. The time 'before' this great event, however, is not merely the same thing but earlier; it is in some way a different order of time-reality, and in some disciplines is not 'former' at all but merely different. It is 'in illo tempore' not 'in priori tempore': in that *other* time, not earlier time.

Australian aborigines believed that time began with a founding drama. This, however, was 'Dream Time', a different order of time, glimpsed in dreams only occasionally. For the Rumanian anthropologist Mircea Eliade, archaic man's lifelong and ever-present concern was to return from profane to mythic time; to begin anew once a year and prevent history starting. For the philosopher Henri Bergson, our real experience is that we inhabit not blank time but succession, duration. This experience of time we have exists in contrast to a hypothetical instant-time in which all reality were present at once. And for Stephen Hawking, in his famous book with its intriguingly inverse title, the lines of time on three fronts (cosmic, psychological, thermodynamic) all go away from the past toward a future we can't attain to, yet might theoretically do in a different universe, or have already done. These diverse notions of time all suggest that the 'Golden Age' myth, even if escapist, nevertheless confronts real elements in the nature of time as we experience it. If only we can get at that other time somehow, the very order of being entailed might bring a solution to all our woes.

The Golden Age myth, familiar enough and common parlance to the Elizabethans, is a poetic embodiment of these ideas. As is commonly known, its earliest surviving expression is in the Greek poet Hesiod, followed by Virgil and then Ovid in the *Metamorphoses*, the work almost certainly used by Shakespeare. Of the four ages – gold, silver, bronze and iron – the cataclysmic event of war between the gods was round about the bronze age, but that still leaves a distinction between gold and silver, which is behind Act II of *As You Like It*.

Harry Levin points out a number of features of the myth which appear in the play. Chief characteristic is that the myth, though a myth, uniquely has no story. Rather, it is a nostalgic state of mind. 'The myth itself has no real protagonist, conceivably because those who dream of it are its truest participants' (1970, p. 27). This absence of story means a dullness of imagery: in effect, says Levin, the oak and the acorn (the latter being etymologically connected to male sex organs – cf. *AYLI* III, ii, 231). It also means, crucially, the emergence of unaggressive woman at the centre. There is equally the theme that the Golden Age and its contact with unsullied nature meant a gentle maturation toward wisdom, and both Levin and Jay Halio in the latter's article on time in *As You Like It* (1962) refer to the 'sermons in stones' speech. This raises the silver-rather-than-gold argument, the fact that Arden does contain the slaughter of deer and indeed 'adversity' for the human inhabitants. The crux is in II, i, 5, 'Here feel we not the penalty of Adam', as Duke Senior puts it, occasioning scholarly disputes as to whether 'not' should read 'but' (= 'merely', 'no worse than').

That would imply that the foresters are in a naturally fallen world, not a full and golden garden of Eden, but one in which, however, at least the horrors of warfare and urban civilisation have not appeared. In short, not golden age but silver, still prior to the cataclysm or flood. There is no rain in Arden as we have said; it is in at least one reading before the flood, whatever else. The argument connects the time theme to the nature–nurture theme, already mentioned, spelt out in Lyly's *Euphues* which greatly influenced Lodge's writing of *Rosalynde*, subtitled *Euphues Golden Legacie*. The view of the young there was that nature itself generates wit, i.e. what we now see as natural genetic endowment. But to the old, wit is a corrupting, 'city-slicker' phenomenon, and the return to nature to attain wit's contrasting wisdom is the right course. That court–country debate also winds through the play, and the return to Arden's golden world is needed for nature's deeper learning to occur and its source to be perceived.

But time in Arden, like so much else, is open to interpretation. By a curious fold-over effect Shakespeare has run different orders and rates of time together. This is because, as said at the start, the characters are banished to Eden, not from it. Put in Golden Age myth terms, the cataclysmic event, here the usurpation of the kingdom and banishment of its rightful holders, sends the characters not from the Golden Age but to it. This gives Shakespeare a certain freedom of manipulation of the time-orders he has none the less invoked by using the time theme at all. On the one hand there is the timeless element itself: no cares, and not really 'rough weather' either, for that certainly doesn't constrain the characters. Orlando specifically tells the Duke that Adam arrives in the forest 'oppress'd with two weak evils, age and hunger' (II, vii, 132); not cold, one notices, which would be his worst enemy if the 'icy fang' of wind the Duke refers to really did bite and blow upon his body.

At the other extreme is exact time-reference amounting to the constraints of duration we push our shoulders against, as Bergson suggested. Jaques's seven ages follow in strict sequence, and we can't reverse them or skip one. What is remarkable, though, is that Jaques's apparently rigid system actually slows the play's movement down. We experience a wait-and-listen feeling while he goes through it. This underscores the ambivalent experience that time is, and points to its greyer areas between the extremes of the timeless and the clock-measured. There are no clocks in this forest, yet the characters refer to fixed hours. Rosalind cannot do without Orlando for two hours, while Touchstone, although lazing in the grass while noting it, sees that eleven follows ten which follows nine, and that while maybe a clock emphasises that further, still we 'ripe and rot' inevitably in that sequence. The first thing Rosalind tells Orlando to hold his attention is the list of four human perceptions of time (III, ii, 302–27). The lover, priest, condemned man and lawyer experience time at different speeds. Rawdon Wilson (1972) has traced the process by which time is perceptibly slowed down and also rendered less drastically switched from court to country as the fugitives arrive in their groups in the forest.

The inferences I would draw from these remarks are, first, that the play includes an awareness of the experience of time as both pressing and casual, and that this is endemic in the ontological experience of time itself. Next, that the play implies latitude in each person's experience of this, perhaps allowing, in a newly individualistic age, some control by humans over how they let such experiences develop. And finally, that Shakespeare himself may have got some therapeutic relief from writing this way, after the 'tyrant time' experience so burdensome in the sonnets, when human relationships were probably burdensome for him too. It enabled the Rosalind phenomenon to grow somewhat away, one imagines, from the Dark Lady. However, as Elton (1986) points out, time as the Elizabethan measurement-conception is in the throes of change, as voyagers and astronomers spread wider and the western hemisphere is discovered. By the time of Milton and Pascal the imagination's dimension is spatial. It may have another colour, as well as gold.

Postmodernism and green space

The timelessness or multiple time of the play, along with its absence of action, renders it largely devoid of historicist narrative, realism or the sociology of traditional community. If it has realism it is magic realism, in Salingar's words 'real people in unreal situations' (1974). Its focus on talk and its great variety of poetic forms make it a writerly not readerly text; it and its characters refer to and display their interest in language itself. It gives off sad irony and gentle laughing parody rather than nightmare or despair. Its absence of soliloquy and discarding of Lodge's 'meditations' mean that self-reflection is not explicit. It is fragmentary in mode, but in the organic way of nature rather than from a past civilisation's rubble. Its very title invokes our multi-cultural focuses, our current 'arguments from difference', and the removal from the artist of critical power. Written between 1593 and 1599 it is *fin de siècle* as we are *fin de millénium*. It has no consumer goods or electronics, yet seems to bask in their benefits, for no work is done, and hunger and fatigue come on the journey to Arden, not on arrival. To us, there is a hint of global warming in its sunlit rainlessness. It has no city, yet court values lie near to the surface of these exiled foresters; the city monolith is nowhere, nor the huge factory or iron army. Its politics are linguistic and sexual; both government and gender relations move through simulacra. All the world's a stage, just as with us all the world's a TV programme. In short, *As You Like It* is postmodern, feminine and green.

It is commonly said that there is a profound anxiety underlying postmodernism. This results from the evident fact of a world past saving, so that one might as well join the pluralist throng and take what is going. As some critics have suggested recently (Davie, 1991, Hebdidge, 1989), the worst side of postmodernism is indeed its consumerism, its flagrant defiant entering of what it might be expected ideologically to reject. The comparable grey strand in *As You Like It* is compounded of the melancholy permanent in Jaques and temporary in Rosalind, and the forest presence, the deep green down in which thought occurs, which is perhaps genitalia and which, at other times, blocks the sunlight out. This is most noticeable in the scenes with Jaques and the Duke, and Oliver's re-entry near the end. It is as though the play stands in relation to Shakespeare's own recent history cycle just as postmodernism stands in relation to the recent collapse of Marxism as a strong force in Western ideology. If it is escapist, perhaps post-modernism is escapist too, a view perhaps held by the many scholars working away at normative historical and literary minutiae, or the behaviour of our play's unmentioned larvae, bacteria and insect life.

And the green element itself, and the epistemological, do seem present in *As You Like It* in a way some of our current literary and cultural reaction rejects. There is little cultural mix in the play, no Jew, Moor or Roman, although the names remind that those Frenchmen (all men) were still linked in a way soon to be reincarnated in our contemporary Britain. Absence of cultural mix may suggest a protectionism or a content with the social order, one I would still argue is no more than a thin and residual motif in the play which is really concerned with other things. We do not know, and are there-fore free to invent, what happened before the play and after it, and whether Duke Frederick was indeed a wicked usurper or Duke Senior a political inept who needed throwing out. (Eagleton, tellingly, hardly touches the play in his revisionary book of 1986.) But Shakespeare's England was under no threat remotely comparable to that of a modern country increasingly layered with motorways, golf courses, technologised parks, leisure centres and wide tourist provision, widespread low-building light industry, international rail and air terminals, and putative new towns – that is to say, where postmodernism's city–country mingling finds the bounds of its actually measur-able territory: the actual, finite planet.

Eagleton, hardly a postmodernist, has yet said in context of
As You Like It, that 'Nature itself produces the means of its
own transformation, contains that which goes beyond it'. To
treat nature as awesomely other 'is just as ideological as it is to
treat it as a moral text in which one can trace one's own sub-
jective moods' (1986, pp. 90–1). In that case Bill McKibben's
The End of Nature (1990) will please Professor Eagleton; but
when years later Shakespeare wrote similar sentiments in *The
Winter's Tale* England still wasn't remotely under such threat
either. I mean simply that, just as Eagleton believes (as we all
do) that it is shameful to see some people fed, technologised
and leisured to the gills while millions starve or are tyrannically
repressed, so too I believe that humans, like animals, need
space around them, including unused space, and including the
case where people spend hours or years in a vast city but still
have psychological easement from stress in knowing that such
wilderness is there. If, inexorably, the planet simply gets used
up by our encroachments and all the world's a garden city (the
garden full of litter, perhaps) then we shall need other, satellite
planets for our wilderness liberty. Otherwise the increase of
our stress and aggression from territorial overcrowding will
increase further as it is increasing now.

Epistemologically, it is worth recalling that Jean-Paul
Lyotard's sub-title for *The Postmodern Condition* was 'A
Report on Knowledge' (1984) and that his enquiry saw that
debate as the starting-point for investigation of our present
dilemmas. Aside from Jaques's desperate attempts to get his
friends into intellectual discussion, *As You Like It* offers
no explicit enquiries into modes of human apprehension of
reality. There is of course the Nature–Wit–Fortune–Folly
debate, as there is the Virtue–Love–Truth–Time debate, but
these fleet the time carelessly, and Rosalind's evident literary
education is cited to ease her own need to guard emotion with
judgement. Yet the general tenor of the play is, I would still
maintain, Aristotelian and Sidneyesque; its indirections are
intended to succeed through delight first. That results in an
emancipation by which deep and pluralist questions can be
asked, scientifically (about animals), morally (about pretence),
philosophically (about truth and language), sociologically and
psychologically (about gender, age-group and occupation),

logically (about mind and wit), metaphysically (about time and space), and aesthetically, about how these other apprehensions are enabled at all. In the absence of actual political actions, murders, rebellions, bureaucracies, institutions, mobs and crowds of citizens, love-poisonings, or even drunken revels as in *Twelfth Night*, masked balls as in *Much Ado About Nothing*, tricks, perfumed barges or games of chess, these more elusive generalities come to the fore of the play unhindered.

Shakespeare's indirection

All of this leads finally to an assessment, however brief, of how the as-you-like-it-ness of the play itself works, and what is its surviving mode of writing and construction. It is commonly held to reside in the way one character says one thing while another seems gently, elsewhere, to deny it; the way different topics intermingle in different ways on different occasions, and the way Shakespeare himself, here even more than elsewhere, 'encompasses more and preaches less than most authors' (Lenz *et al.*, 1983, p. 4). But his adroit or chancy placing of matter in one spot when it 'should' have been at another, his attribution of sayings or actions to the character not centrally associated with such topics, bears equal scrutiny in understanding what is achieved.

Everything is said indirectly. The play never mentions Cain and Abel, yet the biblical strain passing through the play, particularly the centring on an Eden-place, means that once we think of the brother-rivalry ourselves we are unlikely to forget it. The suggestion of the 'old religious uncle' mentioned earlier as Frederick is not alluded to at all, yet since he is indeed Rosalind's uncle we can hardly fail to consider it even if we then reject it. The Rosalind–Orlando love is a fantasy, yet it is Silvius who says all love is fantasy, referring not to them but to himself. There is a curious 'b'-alliteration in the epilogue, which in hindsight links beards, breath and bush as somehow sexually charged, so that the symbol in the latter (as female genitalia) is silently underlined. Of all people Audrey, as already said, asks the crunch questions about poetry's nature, and doesn't know she is raising thereby a whole raft of matters about ugliness and beauty as well as truth and lies. Oliver's remark, ' 'Twas I. But 'tis not I' admirably summarises Rosalind's reappearance.

'Love' goes carefully almost unmentioned in the second wooing scene before Rosalind's 'Leander' speech names it three or four times (IV, i, 89–103), and only the cognate 'lover' is mentioned previously. How extraordinary then that the word should have been used by Jaques, right at the scene's start, but regarding melancholy: 'I do love it better than laughing' (III, i, 4). Jaques 'calls fools into a circle' at II, v, 56 and then seemingly unwittingly echoes this in his own reportage of Touchstone at II, vii, 19, 'Call me not fool, till heaven hath sent me fortune', thus recalling fortune's wheel and its haphazard effects without naming it. Oliver never *says* that he recognises Ganymede as Rosalind at IV, iii, 180, but it is his rather emphatic last word to her after her swooning, despite also having shown at line 92 that he knew 'Rosalind' was Orlando's name for the youth he had met. There are numerous other cases; in fact, one is incessantly being quietly reminded of another aspect of the theme, to which the present reference then seems suddenly subordinate. A central theme (that love-power must displace power-power) is deflected by the huge presence of Jaques's melancholic Act II sandwiched between court government and forest wooing. That 'if' is the big escape-word is told by Touchstone relating how he avoided a duel; and that love may be rendered ideal is masked in that the central lovers don't really actually meet. No character ever refers to what another did earlier on stage, nor declares that one character's words recall another's in agreement or otherwise. The songs perpetuate the themes but subtly altered, and the forest, almost never detailed, is always there.

Perhaps the lasting piece of indirection, however, in a play about love in which the heroine has no body we know about and where no one greatly suffers, not even Phebe, concerns the animal wounded by the hunters before the fugitive lovers even reach the forest, and whose body is described with the blood, fur and tears on it as it dies. The indirection is triple. It introduces Jaques without his being there, it mocks Jaques himself rather than the stag, and it affects to raise a moral issue about the killing of innocent creatures rather than palpably constituting a sexual evocation of body. It is answered, or completed, by the late description by Oliver of Orlando's wounded limbs by another animal, the lioness, the two animals successfully if unknowingly sandwiching the Rosalind–Orlando wooing between them. As the pastoral tradition has implied since Plato's *Phaedrus* and earlier, love idealised occurs in a green world, even if that world is itself sometimes required to surrender its own well-being in the lovers', and their friends', interests. The alternative view is that such love is itself the only hope for regeneration of a world which so exploits its very place of habitation, for such love is the only final locus of the feelings which will show up our less noble activities. Just as you like: the poet affirmes nothing, and therefore never lyeth.

Two things can be said about this. One is that Shakespeare was a 'great artist' in the Renaissance mould who deftly deployed his humanist reading from Castiglione, Montaigne, Erasmus and perhaps Bacon and Ascham, by skilful plotting of language-acts (images, commands, dialogue, songs, characters' words, etc.) so as to achieve a maximum exposure of ideas and issues without ever coming down on one side or another. The other suggestion is that Shakespeare worked at this play on and off, very much collecting bits as he went and putting them in his folder or bottom drawer. A song here, a bit of dialogue there, the useful idea about the world as stage from John of Salisbury elsewhere. Its *bricolage* feel, its lightness of touch feel like that. There was a six-year period within which the play may well have gathered to maturation, if only in Shakespeare's mind. There is much to be said for both these views.

Appendix A:
The major tragedies

In one way or another, aspects of *As You Like It* reappear in the four major tragedies of later years. The play is usually thought to have close association with *King Lear* and, because of the proto-Hamlet figure of Jaques, to have a special interest for *Hamlet*. While not denying these points, I would point to equal interest for *Othello* and *Macbeth* too, especially the latter.

The play has long been associated with *King Lear*. Ornstein (1986, p. 141) sees it as 'a preliminary study for *King Lear*' as a plot summary might suggest. McCombie (1980) calls the later play *As You Like It Not*, the same play rewritten six years later but through the filter of tragedy rather than comedy. Maynard Mack (1966) was early in elaborating the main ingredients: a ruler and his daughter, and a subplot of faithful follower and his two sons. Furthermore, unlike in some plays main plot and subplot are integrated throughout. Added to all this are more parallels, too numerous to do more than mention here but given in detail in McCombie. Duke Frederick is like the unregenerate Lear, Duke Senior the more regenerate. Celia and Edgar both brown their faces for disguise; Oliver's ejection and the confiscation of his estates is what happens to Gloucester;

Old Adam precurses the old gentleman who assists Gloucester when blinded. Most of all there is the parallel between the fools Touchstone and Lear's Fool, both of whom echo Erasmus rather closely, and both of whom have known better times but remain loyal. The raging speech of Lear himself, 'blow winds, and crack your cheeks', takes forward the earlier play's song 'blow, blow, thou winter wind'. And Lear of course rages against 'this great stage of fools', which stage Jaques had elaborated on more lengthily, though it is never far from any of the tragedies. In closer detail still: eyes, snails and civets figure far more prominently in both plays than elsewhere in Shakespeare.

The suggestion is not merely that Shakespeare wrote a new play on an old theme but that he seldom had *As You Like It* far from his mind at the time. This cannot be pursued further here but two points stand out. One is that Lear has a far greater degree of purgation to endure – quite aside from Cordelia's death – than Duke Senior is depicted as experiencing. The second is that Lear evinces the greatest revulsion against sex that Shakespeare expressed anywhere, and this really is remarkable if held to have been occasioned by a play as sexually subtle yet largely unbawdy as *As You Like It*. The common element is probably nature itself, and the change from a beneficent nature in the comedy to a hostile one in the tragedy; yet this is hardly a satisfactory account of what is, of course, a real parallel.

James Smith and Jan Kott were among the immediate post-war critics who took up the traditional association of Jaques with Hamlet. Smith (1974) suggests that Hamlet speaks with true disgust while Jaques does not, and further that Hamlet cannot be *betrayed* into action, while Jaques could. This points to the original line of connection between them: not merely the cynicism or disgust, but the incapacity for action. Jaques of course is depicted, however, as a former libertine, then disgusted with the world (perhaps an exaggerated picture of Lyly's old age, though Marston is more often cited). Jan Kott is more intriguing on the subject. He suggests (1967, pp. 230–1) that to prefigure Hamlet Jaques must be a man, and have a personal reason for his bitterness. To be just an Elizabethan melancholic or malcontent would have been insufficient. As a result, Jaques begins to envy Touchstone his fool's motley just as Hamlet, if with more detachment and self-knowledge, eyes the players at Elsinore with some wistful envy. But Jaques is an intrusion into Arden, as into Lodge's story, and he alone remains there at the end. Furthermore it is not only Jaques who talks of what Hamlet later calls 'this stale, unprofitable world'. Orlando says something comparable, and with some self-abasement at ii, iii, 56ff., as indeed did Rosalind at i, iii, 11–12. In *Hamlet* the prince of Denmark moves centre stage, as though perhaps Jaques's absorption with the theatre as world-image led Shakespeare to want to elaborate the whole idea by using the play-within-a-play motif as focus for his protagonist's inner agonies.

Othello is a rather different case. It is often thought of as preceded in Shakespeare's mind by *Measure For Measure*. But there are one or two curious parallels with our play. One is the double-time element, which is more metaphysical in *As You Like It*, more a straight difference of time-scales in the tragedy. In Act ii of *As You Like It* there is a discrepancy between the 'new news at the new court', implying the Duke's banishment was recent, and Celia's reference to the same banishment as occurring when 'I was too young that time to value her' (i, iii, 67; i.e. Rosalind, now to be banished herself), implying a fair period of development. The debate about the phrase 'old custom' at the start of Act ii adds to the uncertainty. Yet all of this fits within a much more pervading theme of multifarious time, as we have seen. But in *Othello* the double-time scheme has a mainly dramatic function. The details are spelt out in Ridley's introduction to the play in the Arden edition (1958).

Briefly: on the one hand the action must move very rapidly, otherwise Iago's diabolical scheme will be spotted; the drama depends on this very thing. Yet that very speed makes the story in literal terms a nonsense, for there is no conceivable moment in the play when Desdemona's supposed adultery could have occurred. Shakespeare solves the problem skilfully by suggesting long-term events quickly in passing, as it were hoping the audience won't notice.

But if there is a deeper implication in *Othello* behind the double-time it can surely only be that Othello ought himself to have realised the adultery was impossible and that Shakespeare meant us to see that. This can't be considered here, but it takes us back to *As You Like It*. For, as well as the oft-remarked similarity – though hardly developed – between Iago and Oliver, more notable surely is the way that Iago's extended dangling and tricking of Othello is not dissimilar to Rosalind's prolonged deception of Orlando. Each spreads over two acts and has certain distinct stages. What is more, *each ends in a mock-marriage*. O'Neill (1984) has shown how Act iii, scene iii ends in a kind of travesty of the marriage service, Iago's last words being 'I am your own for ever'. Of course, the entire tenor of Rosalind's actions, whatever one's critical persuasion, is in an obvious general sense positive and loving, and Iago's sinister embroilment of entirely innocent people in wounding, dishonour and death is quite absent from Arden forest. Yet what we said earlier about Orlando's possible androgyny, and the undeniable element of deception right through Rosalind's disguise, does make one ask whether the ever-adaptive Shakespeare may not have found seeds in the earlier work, or his preparation for it, which became absorbed in the later tragedy. In *Othello* early on, Brabantio warns Othello about Desdemona: 'Look to her, Moor, have a quick eye to see,/ She has deceived her father, may do thee'. But Rosalind does just those two things. She keeps her identity back from her father (*As You Like It* iii, iv, 31–5) and, of course, 'deceives' Orlando. The implication is not a backward suspicious glance at Rosalind; rather, it is a look into Shakespeare's thinking over the years of his career; his endless transformation and recombination of human, poetic and dramatic possibilities.

In *Macbeth* there seem to me perhaps the most interesting parallels and contrast with *As You Like It*, albeit seldom remarked. Like the comedy, *Macbeth* is much about truth and lies. The new word here, however, is 'equivocation'; yet the essence is the same. As in *Lear* Macbeth dwells in a rugged and hostile landscape, in which he meets three weird sisters. These women are, perhaps, a transposition, in Shakespeare's time of sexual disgust, of some of the brilliant creative women of the comedies. They deceive Macbeth, as Rosalind deceives both her father and her lover, but in this case by the insidious method of making prophecies literally true but false in spirit and intention. Current critical opinion does not entirely fault the three sisters as it used to. They are not the 'wicked witches' as they traditionally were, or not as uncompromisingly so. They too can be taken as allegorical for females under the yoke of the ambition of such as Macbeth. The emphasis on the worst aspect, however – lie as half-truth, trick-truth – remains; these are 'fiends that lie like truth', as Macbeth says, defeated at the end and awakening to what has been done to him.

But all of this is inseparable, of course, from the prophecy of the apparition Macbeth sees, during thunder, in Act iv, scene i of the play, 'a child crowned, with a tree in his hand'. The prophecy is that Macbeth will 'never vanquish'd be, until/ Great Birnam wood to high Dunsinane hill/ Shall come against him'. This equivocating mix of truth and lie ties that truth-problem right in with the deepest vibrations of the 'green' theme of *As You Like It*, the forest of Arden. The eternal certainty of woodland nature itself is shifting. Touchstone's 'Let the forest judge' cannot, in effect, ever be relied on again. Again this cannot be examined here in detail, but rival inter-pretations of *Macbeth* do not remove the implication. If the witches and apparitions are imaginary, then Macbeth himself is irreversibly cut off from nature's sustaining power and re-newal, and this is at the heart of the tragedy. But if they are real visitors from some nightmare other world, then they would appear to control nature themselves. Either way, the fact remains that at practical level the wood does move; not quite as devastatingly, yet, as our rain-forests do when we slash them down, but to such extent at least to give the impression of a whole wood uprooted or diabolically energised.

This seems to be as drastic a suggestion of change of attitude in Shakespeare to nature as that found in *Lear*. The green drama of the early plays has surrendered its place as deepest guarantor of our planetary peace and domestication. It is not now that the tragic characters have been banished from Eden; it seems rather that Eden itself has been banished, either by evil supernatural forces or, just as alarmingly, by the tragedy of disturbed minds. It is some relief to return to *As You Like It* and find it as reassuring as ever; for Shakespeare the new step was on, to the grey and thoughtful yet ultimately reconciling seascapes of the late romances.

Appendix B:
Terms

(All information given here comes from the Oxford English Dictionary.)

This is not an exhaustive list; simply certain words I gradually found myself wanting to check up, because their meanings seemed able to allow, even require, interesting possibilities of meaning in the play.

Adolescent (not in, but a kind of pun on 'as you like it', rather like 'Master What-ye-call't' for 'Jaques', III, iii, 66). Adolescence is 'the period which extends from childhood to manhood' – *OED*. Used by Lydgate, *Bochas* (1430), IX, xxv: 'afterward is their Adolescence Vertuously to teach them'. In other words, it just could have been a pun, or echo.

Bottom 'My affection hath an unknown bottom, like the Bay of Portugal' (IV, i, 197–8). Not used for human posterior until Erasmus Darwin in 1794, according to *OED*. But 'bottom of sea, deep place or abyss', etc., go back to Beowulf and Caedmon. 'Lowest part of anything' (e.g. keel of ship, bottom of bottle) also back to Caedmon. 'Fundamental character or essence': first refs are late sixteenth century (including Tourneur, 1600), around in Shakespeare's time;

e.g. Harrison (1577): 'when the pope understood the botome of the matter'. An example from 1594 cited in *OED* is 'there is nothing in man which God searcheth not vnto the bottome'.

Come   (cf. Juliet's speech in *R&J* III, ii, 1–31). Not sexual orgasm until 1650: 'then off he came, and blusht for shame soe soone that he had endit' (*Walking on the Green*). But possibly predisposing connotations (to germinate, put forth the radicle, come into existence, appear on surface of body, grow, etc.) back to *c.* 1400, and butter 'coming' (congealing) in the churn, 1577.

Fleet   *OED* cites the *AYLI* passage (I, i, 118) as first case of meaning 'while away the time'. Prior were to overrun, over-flow (Phillips, 1598), vanish, fade away (*MofV* III, ii, 108 and generally in Spenser, Lyly *Euphues* etc.). Also to move unsteadily, flow, stream, glide, 1580s and 1590; Spenser, *Colin Clout*, 1. 596; many references to second half of 1590s decade. Shakespeare seems to have pinpointed this meaning. I think it is more than just 'while away'. There is a transitive connotation: wallow in, enjoy, set afloat, even assemble.

Humorous   According to *OED*, humorous as a) damp, b) subject to mood, c) peevish, *out* of humour, *begins* with Shakespeare. First refs given in *OED* are, respectively, *R&J* II, i, 31, *LLL* III, i, 177 and *AYLI* I, ii, 256 ('the duke is humorous'). The older meaning, as one of the four fluids (blood, choler, phlegm, melancholy) goes back at least to the sermons of Wyclif in 1380. This comes of course from medieval physiology. The traditional meaning of general disposition, state of mind, is common in the 1590s, indeed begins only a little earlier. 'Humorous' as funny, openly amusing, doesn't come till the early eight-eenth century. *But* humorous as facetious, jocular, appears around 1600 (Chettles, 1603; Cotgrave, 1611), and it is this meaning I think that could be attached to the Duke Frederick.

It ('As You Like It')   *OED* gives the sexual intercourse mean-ing, but first case is 1611, Cotgrave's *Dictionary*: for *fretiller* 'to lust, to be at'; cf. of course in *Lear* IV, vi, 115, 'the wren goes to 't, and the small gilded fly/ Does lecher in my sight'. ('It' surely doesn't refer back to 'adultery' in previous line, or 'copulation' in 'let copulation thrive'; it is a more general 'it', meaning sex itself but not via the particular noun's attraction.)

Jakes Can be spelt *jacques* or *jaques* in its 'privy' meaning too, as well as the name, from the 1530s on. Cf. e.g.
Harrington (1596) (*OED* reference).

Jars

> If he, compact of jars, grow musical,
> We shall have shortly discord in the spheres
>
> (II, vii, 5–6)

Discord as 'a harsh unharmonious sound', comes in at about
1520 (Skelton, Udall *et al.*) and *OED* cites this passage from
AYLI, as well as Drayton (1598). (It could also mean the
ticking of a clock: *RII* v, v, 51; *WT* I, ii, 43.) But I had
wondered if it could mean a pint of beer, as now – 'fancy a
jar?' (because Richard Pasco's Jaques in the BBC TV version
has him plastered when Orlando arrives with old Adam).
But that meaning doesn't come until the twentieth century
(Sean O'Casey). Rather, it *could* mean disputes, quarrels
(Babington, 1583), and Duke Senior and Jaques have been
sniping at each other, each calling the other disputatious
while denying it himself (II, i, 67–8; II, v, 31–2). However, 'vessel' (earthenware, glass, etc.) is earliest in Hakluyt
(1592). So the pun is there.

Lie As in false statement, goes back to Bede. Many cases in
sixteenth century, then also *MofV* III, iv, 71. As in sexual
intercourse, *OED* says 'somewhat arch'. But it goes back to
Mandeville, Malory and others. Euphemism from lying in
bed, sleeping with, etc. Not all that common, but cf. *Othello*
(not cited in *OED*): 'lie . . . with her, on her, what you will'
(*Othello* IV, i, 32–4; note incidentally the *TN* subtitle echo).
Various spots in *AYLI*: truth *and* love.

Natural A disappointingly dull entry! – not the *OED*'s fault,
of course. Taking place in ordinary course of things: not
exceptional: physical not spiritual: not artificial: according
to operation of natural laws: simple, inherent, unaffected –
all found in the sixteenth century or a bit earlier. So the
AYLI reference, which might have allowed a lesbian connotation between Rosalind and Celia, is certainly not
necessary, and might seem unlikely:

> To keep his daughter company, whose loves
> Are dearer than the natural bond of sisters.
>
> (I, ii, 265–6)

However, its opposite, 'unnatural', often meant not merely unexpected, but disturbingly so: monstrous, cruel, devoid of proper feeling, illegitimate, strange, distorted; *against* nature (Gosson, *The School Of Abuse*, 1579; Sidney, *Arcadia*, 1586). Cf. *Macbeth* II, iv, 10. So, 'dearer than . . .' could be at least pointed (though, of course, perhaps pointedly *away* from the undesirable meaning).

Page   As boy in training, etc., from early in the fourteenth century – but not 'to wait on, attend' as verb until 1596 (cf. also *Timon* IV, iii, 224). And page of book is first recorded in 1589 – also relatively recent at time of *AYLI* – in Nashe's Preface to Greene's *Menaphon*. So the 'banished Duke's pages' (*AYLI* V, iii, 5), Touchstone's reference to the two young singers, could also be a pun reference to censorship, fairly prevalent in the Elizabethan period (cf. I, ii, 82–4).

Wit   'Wit whither wilt?': was a phrase addressed to people when they were letting their tongues run away with them. Often taken to illustrate Orlando's poor attempt at wit, but, if the *OED* is correct, this instance (IV, i, 157–8) is the first occasion of such a use. Later *OED* citings include Greene (1617), Middleton (1623) and Heywood (1637).

Wit as good or great mental capacity: mental quickness and acumen: genius, talent, ingenuity, skill, cleverness, discretion, wisdom – all go back to the fourteenth century and earlier. Aptness of thought or expression, however, the unexpected phrase, tends to come in the later seventeenth century, and the power to say 'brilliant or sparkling things in an unusual way' (*OED*) is later still, into the eighteenth century. Theme throughout play, of course, not just here.

Wisdom   By contrast, a cognate word, is the 'capacity of judging right, soundness of judgement in choice of ends or means' and goes back to Beowulf. It is 'opposed to folly' (*sic*), but the suggestion of wisdom as entailing the thoughtful silence that stems from much experience, is not given.

Bibliography

Text

Shakespeare, William, *As You Like It*, ed. Agnes Lathem, London: Methuen, The Arden Shakespeare, 1975.

All references to other plays of Shakespeare are from the Arden Shakespeare editions, Methuen & Co. Ltd, various editors. Also 'As You Like It' produced by Cedric Messina, in the BBC TV Shakespeare Series.

Other reading

Anon., 'Hic Mulier' and 'Haec-Vir', *The Rota*, University of Exeter, 1973.

Armstrong, Isobel, 'Thatcher's Shakespeare?', *Textual Practice*, vol. 3, no. 1, Spring 1989, pp. 1–14.

Bacon, Francis, *Essays* (Introduction by Michael J. Hawkins), London: Dent, 1972.

Bamber, Linda, *Comic Women, Tragic Men: A study of gender and genre in Shakespeare*, Stanford: University of California Press, 1982.

Barber, C.L., *Shakespeare's Festive Comedy: A study of dramatic form and its relation to social custom*, New Jersey: Princeton University Press, 1959.

Bartholomeusz, Dennis, 'Shakespeare on the Melbourne stage', *Shakespeare Survey* 35 (1982), pp. 31–41.

Bate, Jonathan, *Shakespeare and the English Romantic Imagination*, Oxford: Clarendon Press, 1989.

Beckman, Margaret Boemer, 'The figure of Rosalind in "As You Like It"', *Shakespeare Quarterly* 29 (1978), pp. 44–51.

Bergson, Henri, *Creative Evolution*, London: Macmillan, 1911.

Berndt, Catherine H., 'Women and the secret life', in *Aboriginal Man in Australia: Essays in honour of Professor A.P. Elkin*, ed. R.M. Berndt and C.H. Berndt, London: Angus & Robertson, 1965.

Berry, Ralph, *Shakespeare's Comedies*, New Jersey: Princeton University Press, 1972.

Brockbank, Philip, *Players of Shakespeare*, Cambridge University Press, 1985.

Brown, Ivor, *Shakespeare*, London: Collins, Fontana Books, 1949.

Brown, John Russell, *Shakespeare and his Comedies*, London: Methuen University Paperback, 1973.

Brown, John Russell, *Shakespeare: Much Ado About Nothing and As You Like It*, Basingstoke: Macmillan, Casebook Series, 1979.

Bullough, Geoffrey, *Narrative and Dramatic Sources of Shakespeare*, vol. II *The Comedies 1597–1603*, London: Routledge & Kegan Paul, 1958.

Burton, Robert, *The Anatomy of Melancholy*, ed. Holbrook Jackson, London: Dent, 1932.

Callow, Simon, *Being an Actor*, Harmondsworth: Penguin Books, 1984.

Castiglione, Baldesar, *The Book of the Courtier* (trans. George Bull), Harmondsworth: Penguin Classics, 1967.

Chambers, E.K., *Shakespeare: A survey*, London: Sidgwick & Jackson, 1925.

Charlton, H.B., *Shakespearian Comedy*, London: Methuen, 1938.

Coleridge, S.T., *Shakespeare Criticism*, ed. T.M. Raynor, London: Dent, 1960.

Coleridge, S.T., *Coleridge on Shakespeare* (text of the 1811–12 lectures), ed. R. A. Foakes, London: Routledge & Kegan Paul, 1971.

Davie, Donald, 'Postmodernism and Alan Curnow', *Poetry Nation Review*, 17 (1991), pp. 31–41.

Davies, W. Robertson, *Shakespeare's Boy Actors*, London: Dent, 1939.

Docherty, Thomas, *On Moral Authority: The Theory and Conditions of Writing: 1500 to the Present Day*, Brighton: Harvester, 1987.

Dowden, Edward, *Shakspere: A critical study of his mind and art*, London: Henry S. King & Co., 1875.

Dowden, Edward, Introduction to 'As You Like It' in *The Comedies of Shakespeare*, ed. W. J. Craik, Oxford University Press, 1911, pp. 667–9.

Dusinberre, Juliet, *Shakespeare and the Nature of Women*, Basingstoke: Macmillan, 1975.

Eagleton, Terry, *William Shakespeare*, Oxford: Blackwell, 1986.

Easlea, Brian, *Witch-hunting, Magic and the New Philosophy*, Brighton: Harvester, 1980.

Elam, Keir, *Shakespeare's Universe of Discourse: Language-games in the comedies*, Cambridge University Press, 1984.

Eliade, Mircea, *The Myth of the Eternal Return: Cosmos and history* (trans. Willard R. Trask), London: Penguin, 1989.

Elton, W.R., 'Shakespeare and the thought of his age', in *The Cambridge Companion to Shakespeare Studies*, ed. Stanley Wells, Cambridge University Press, 1986, pp. 17–34.

Erasmus, Desiderius, *In Praise of Folly* (trans. Betty Radice), Harmondsworth: Penguin Classics, 1971.

Ettore, E.M., *Lesbians, Women and Society*, London: Routledge & Kegan Paul, 1980.

Evans, Bertrand, *Shakespeare's Comedies*, Oxford: Clarendon Press, 1960.

Evans, Malcolm, *Signifying Nothing: Truth's true contents in Shakespeare's text*, Brighton: Harvester, 1986.

Everett, Barbara, 'The fatness of Falstaff – Shakespeare's characters' (British Academy Shakespeare Lecture, 24 April 1990).

Faucit, Helena, *Shakespeare's Female Characters*, Edinburgh & London: Blackwood, 1841.

Felperin, Howard, *Shakespearian Romance*, New Haven, CT: Yale University Press, 1970.

Foucault, Michel, *The History of Sexuality*, vol. 1 (trans. Robert Hurley), London: Allen Lane, 1979.

Foulkes, Richard (ed.), *Shakespeare and the Victorian Stage*, Cambridge University Press, 1986.

French, Marilyn, *Shakespeare's Division of Experience*, London: Abacus (Sphere Books), 1983.

Frye, Northrop, *The Anatomy of Criticism*, New Jersey: Princeton University Press, 1957.

Frye, Northrop, 'The argument of comedy' in *Shakespeare: Modern essays in criticism*, ed. Leonard F. Dean, Oxford University Press, 1967, pp. 79–89.

Gardner, Helen, 'As You Like It', in *More Talking of Shakespeare*, ed. John Garrett, London: Longmans, 1959, pp. 17–32.

Gautier, Theophile, *Mademoiselle de Maupin*, ed. Joanna Richardson, London: Penguin Books, 1981.

Gittings, Robert, *Young Thomas Hardy*, Harmondsworth: Penguin, 1978.

Gosse, Sir Edmund, 'Thomas Lodge', in *Seventeenth Century Studies*, London: Kegan Paul & Trench, 1883.

Greenblatt, Stephen, *Shakespearian Negotiations: The circulation of social energy in Renaissance England*, Oxford: Clarendon Press, 1988.

Halio, Jay L., ' "No clock in the forest": Time in "As You Like It" ', in *Studies in English Literature*, vol. ii, Spring 1962, no. 2, pp. 197–207.

Harbage, Alfred, *Shakespeare's Audience*, New York: Columbia University Press, 1941.

Hayles, Nancy K. 'Sexual disguise in "As You Like It" and "Twelfth Night" ', *Shakespeare Survey* 32 (1979), pp. 63–72.

Hazlitt, William, *Characters of Shakespeare's Plays*, London: Taylor & Hessey, 1818.

Hebdidge, Dick, 'The bottom line on Planet One', in *Ten 8*, no. 19 (1989), pp. 40–9.

Holden, Anthony, *Olivier*, London: Sphere Books, 1988.

Holding, Edith, ' "As You Like It" adapted: Charles Johnson's *Love In A Forest*', *Shakespeare Survey* 32 (1979), pp. 37–48.

Holland, Norman N., *Psychoanalysis and Shakespeare*, New York: McGraw-Hill, 1964.

Hooker, Richard, *Of the Laws of Ecclesiastical Polity*, University of Chicago Press, n.d. (reprint of Clarendon Press edition, 1890).

Hoskins, W.G., *The Making of the English Landscape*, Harmondsworth: Penguin, 1955.

Houghton, Walter E., *The Victorian Frame of Mind*, New Haven, CT: Yale University Press, 1957.

Howard, Jean E., 'Crossdressing, the theatre and gender struggle in early modern England', *Shakespeare Quarterly* 39 (1988), pp. 418–40.

Hudson, Derek, *Lewis Carroll*, London: Constable, 1954.

Hunter, G.K., *John Lyly*, London: Routledge & Kegan Paul, 1962a.

Hunter, G.K., *Shakespeare: The late comedies*, London: Longmans, Green & Co. (*Writers and Their Work* series), 1962b.

Jackson, Russell, ' "Perfect types of womanhood": Rosalind, Beatrice and Viola in Victorian criticism and performance', *Shakespeare Survey* 32 (1979), pp. 15–26.

Jameson, Anna, *Characteristics of Women, Moral, Political and Historical*, vol. i, London: Saunders & Otley, 1832.

Jardine, Lisa, *Still Harping on Daughters*, Brighton: Harvester, 1983.

Jenkins, Elizabeth, *Jane Austen*, London: Gollancz, 1961.

Jenkins, Harold, '*As You Like It*' in *Shakespeare: Modern essays in criticism*, ed. Leonard F. Dean, Oxford University Press, 1967, pp. 114–33.

Johnson, Paul, *Elizabeth 1*, London: Weidenfeld & Nicolson, 1974.

Johnson, Samuel, 'Preface to Shakespeare' and 'Notes on the plays' in *Johnson on Shakespeare*, ed. W. Ralegh, Oxford University Press, 1908.

Kitzinger, Celia, *The Social Construction of Lesbianism*, London: Sage Editions, 1987.

Kott, Jan, *Shakespeare Our Contemporary*, London: Methuen, 1967.

Kreiger, Elliot, *A Marxist Study of Shakespeare's Comedies*, London: Macmillan, 1979.

Kronenfeld, Judy Z., 'Social rank and the pastoral ideals of "As You Like It"', *Shakespeare Quarterly* 29 (1978), pp. 333–48.

Laslett, Peter, *The World We Have Lost*, London: Methuen, 1965.

Leggatt, Alexander, *Shakespeare's Comedy of Love*, London and New York: Methuen, 1974.

Lenz, C.R.S., G. Greene and C.T. Neely, *The Woman's Part: Feminist criticism of Shakespeare*, Urbana and Chicago: University of Illinois Press, 1983.

Levin, Harry, *The Myth of the Golden Age in the Renaissance*, London: Faber, 1970.

Levin, Richard, 'Women in the Renaissance theatre audience', *Shakespeare Quarterly* 40 (1989), pp. 165–74.

Lifson, Martha Ronk, 'Learning by talking: conversation in "As You Like It"', *Shakespeare Survey* 40 (1987), pp. 91–105.

Lodge, Thomas, *Rosalynde. Euphues Golden Legacie*, London: George Newnes Ltd, 1902.

Lyly, John, *Euphues: The anatomy of wit*, in *The Complete Works of John Lyly*, ed. R. Warwick Bond, Oxford: Clarendon Press, 1902, vol. 1, pp. 172–326.

Lyotard, Jean-François, *The Postmodern Condition: A report on knowledge* (trans. G. Bemington and G. Massumi), Manchester: Manchester University Press, 1984.

McCombie, Frank, 'Medium and message in "As You Like It" and "King Lear"', *Shakespeare Survey* 33 (1980), pp. 67–80.

McFarland, Thomas, *Shakespeare's Pastoral Comedy*, Chapel Hill, NC: University of North Carolina Press, 1972.

Macfarlane, Alan, *The Origins of English Individualism*, Oxford: Blackwell, 1978.

McKibben, Bill, *The End of Nature*, Harmondsworth: Penguin Books, 1990.

Machiavelli, Niccolò, *The Prince* (trans. W.K. Marriott), London: Dent, 1958.

Mack, Maynard, *King Lear in Our Time*, London: Methuen, 1966.

Mackenzie, Agnes M., *The Women in Shakespeare's Plays*, London: Heinemann, 1924.

Marlowe, Christopher, *Hero and Leander*, in *The Complete Plays and Poems*, ed. Stephen Orgel, Harmondsworth: Penguin Classics, 1971.

Marowitz, Charles, 'Reconstructing Shakespeare or harlotry in bardolatry', *Shakespeare Survey* 40 (1987), pp. 1–10.

Martin, Sir Theodore, *Helena Faucit, Lady Martin*, Edinburgh & London: Blackwood, 1900.

Millgate, Michael, *Thomas Hardy*, Oxford University Press, 1982.

Montague, Elizabeth, *Correspondence 1720–1761*, vol. 1, ed. Emily Climenson, London: John Murray, 1906.

Montaigne, Michel de, *Essays* (trans. J. M. Cohen), Harmondsworth: Penguin Classics, 1958.

Nangesser, Lon G., *Homosexual Acts, Actors and Identities*, New York: Praeger Studies, 1983.

Nevo, Ruth, *Comic Transformations in Shakespeare*, London & New York: Methuen, 1980.

O'Connor, Garry, *Ralph Richardson: An actor's life*, London: Hodder & Stoughton, 1982.

O'Neill, Michael, 'Changing places in *Othello*', *Shakespeare Survey* 37 (1984), pp. 115–31.

Ornstein, Robert, *Shakespeare's Comedies: From Roman farce to romantic mystery*, Newark: University of Delaware Press, 1986.

Park, Clara Clairborne, 'As we like it: how a girl can be smart and still popular', in *The Woman's Part: Feminist criticism of Shakespeare*, ed. C.R. Swift Lenz, G. Greene and C.T. Neely, Urbana, IL: University of Illinois Press, 1983, pp. 100–16.

Potts, Abbie Findlay, *Shakespeare and The Faerie Queene*, Ithaca, NY: Cornell University Press, 1958.

Raby, Peter, *Fair Ophelia: A life of Harriet Smithson Berlioz*, Cambridge University Press, 1982.

Racksin, Phyllis, 'Androgyny, mimesis and the marriage of the boy héroine on the English Renaissance stage', in *Speaking of Gender*, ed. E. Showalter, London: Routledge & Kegan Paul, 1989, pp. 113–33.

Ralegh, Walter, *Shakespeare*, London: Macmillan, Morley's Men of Letters Series, 1907.

Reynolds, Peter, *As You Like It*, Harmondsworth: Penguin Books (Penguin Critical Studies), 1988.

Roberts, Jeanne Addison, 'Making a woman and other institutionalized diversions', *Shakespeare Quarterly* 37 (1986), pp. 366–9.

Rosenberg, Marvin, 'Sign theory and Shakespeare', *Shakespeare Survey* 40 (1987), pp. 33–40.

Rowse, A. L., *Shakespeare The Man*, St Albans: Granada Paladin, 1976.

Rubinstein, Frankie, *A Dictionary of Shakespeare's Sexual Puns and Their Significance*, Basingstoke: Macmillan, 1984.

Salgado, Gamini, *Eye-witnesses of Shakespeare*, Brighton: Sussex University Press, 1975.

Salingar, L.G., 'The social setting', in *The Age of Shakespeare*, ed. Boris Ford, Harmondsworth: Pelican Guide To English Literature, 1955, vol II, pp. 15–47.

Salingar, L.G., *Shakespeare and the Traditions of Comedy*, Cambridge University Press, 1974.

Salingar, L.G., 'Jacobean playwrights and "judicious" spectators' in *Proceedings of the British Academy* LXXV, 1989, pp. 1–23.

Schegloff, E. and H. Sacks, 'Opening up closings', in *Ethnomethodology*, ed. Roy Turner, Harmondsworth: Penguin Education, 1974, pp. 233–64.

Seng, Peter J., *The Vocal Songs in the Plays of Shakespeare*, Cambridge, MA: Harvard University Press, 1967.

Seymour-Smith, Martin (ed.), *Shakespeare's Sonnets*, London: Heinemann, 1963.

Showalter, Elaine, 'The rise of gender', in *Speaking of Gender*, ed. E. Showalter, London: Routledge & Kegan Paul, 1989, pp. 1–17.

Sidney, Sir Philip, *An Apologie for Poetrie*, in *The Prelude to Poetry*, ed. Ernest Rhys, London: Dent, 1927.

Sidney, Sir Philip, *The Countess of Pembroke's Arcadia*, ed. Maurice Evans, Harmondsworth: Penguin English Library, 1977.

Simmel, Georg, *The Sociology of Georg Simmel* (trans. Kurt H. Wolff), London: Collier-Macmillan, 1950, and Free Press of Glencoe.

Smith, Irwin, *Shakespeare's Globe Playhouse: A modern reconstruction*, New York: Charles Scribner's, 1956.

Smith, Irwin, *Shakespeare's Blackfriars Playhouse*, New York: University Press, 1964.

Smith, James, 'As You Like It', in *Shakespeare and Other Essays*, Cambridge University Press, 1974, pp. 1–23.

Sprague, Arthur Colby, *Shakespearian Players and Performances*, London: A & C Black, 1954.

Stanner, W.E.H., 'Religion, totemism and symbolism', in *Aboriginal Man in Australia: Essays in honour of Professor A.P. Elkin*, ed. R.M. Berndt and C.H. Berndt, London: Angus & Robertson, 1965.

Stevenson, Juliet *et al.*, 'Rosalind: iconoclast in Arden', in *Clamorous Voices*, ed. Faith Evans; interviews by Carol Rutter, London: The Woman's Press, 1988, pp. 97–121.

Swinburne, Algernon Charles, *A Study of Shakespeare*, London: Chatto & Windus, 1880.

Thomas, Edward, *Selected Prose*, ed. Edna Longley, Manchester: Carcanet, 1981.

Thomas, Keith, *Man and the Natural World: Changing attitudes in England 1500–1800*, London: Allen Lane, 1983.

Vickers, Brian, *Shakespeare: The critical heritage*, vols. ii–vi, London: Routledge & Kegan Paul, 1974–81.

Weeks, Jeffery, *Sexuality and its Discontents*, London: Routledge & Kegan Paul, 1985.

Wells, Stanley (ed.), *The Cambridge Companion to Shakespeare Studies*, Cambridge University Press, 1986, pp. 17–34.

Wilcher, Robert, 'The art of the comic duologue in three plays by Shakespeare', *Shakespeare Survey* 35 (1982), pp. 87–100.

Wilson, J. Dover (with A. Quiller-Couch), Introduction to 'As You Like It', Arden edition, Cambridge University Press, 1926.

Wilson, Rawdon, 'The way to Arden: attitudes toward time in "As You Like It"', *Shakespeare Quarterly* 23 (1972), pp. 16–24.

Winnicott, D.W., *Playing and Reality*, Harmondsworth: Penguin Education, 1974.

Wolk, Antony, 'The extra Jaques in "As You Like It"', *Shakespeare Quarterly* 23 (1972), pp. 101–5.

Wrightson, Keith, *English Society 1580–1680*, London: Hutchinson, 1982.

Young, David, *The Heart's Forest: A study of Shakespeare's pastoral plays*, New Haven, CT: Yale University Press, 1972.

Reviews of Shakespeare in performance

Shakespeare Quarterly 23 (1972); 29 (1978), pp. 225–6; 237–8; 261–2; 37 (1986); 38 (1987).

Shakespeare Survey 34 (1981); 39 (1987).

Index